ALTHEA GIBSON

Illustrated by Meryl Henderson

ALTHEA GIBSON
Young Tennis Player

by Beatrice Gormley

ALADDIN PAPERBACKS

New York London Toronto Sydney

ALADDIN PAPERBACKS
An imprint of Simon & Schuster Children's Publishing Division
1230 Avenue of the Americas, New York, NY 10020
Text copyright © 2005 by Beatrice Gormley
Illustrations copyright © 2005 by Meryl Henderson
All rights reserved, including the right of reproduction in
whole or in part in any form.
ALADDIN PAPERBACKS and colophon are registered trademarks
of Simon & Schuster, Inc.
Designed by Lisa Vega
The text of this book was set in New Caledonia.
Manufactured in the United States of America
First Aladdin Paperbacks edition January 2005
2 4 6 8 10 9 7 5 3 1
Library of Congress Control Number 2004105710
ISBN 0-689-87187-2

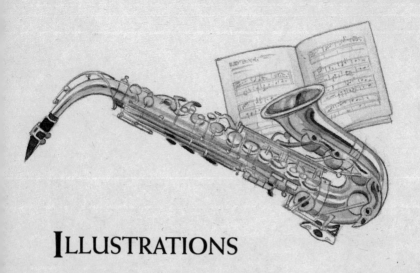

ILLUSTRATIONS

CONTENTS

A Little Champ

The sun hung low over the cotton fields. In Clarendon County, South Carolina, it was the end of a summer day in 1930. A young man, Daniel "Dush" Gibson, plodded out of the white-tufted cotton bushes. The rows of cotton ran up almost to the Gibsons' cabin, but there was a bare space in front of the porch. A tall oak tree shaded the dirt and the chickens that pecked in it.

A young woman, Annie Gibson, stepped down from the cabin porch to meet him. She carried a baby on her hip. "Dush, I'm glad you're home. Althea's been pestering and pestering."

A three-year-old girl darted out from behind her mother and threw herself into her father's arms. "Daddy, Daddy!"

A smile spread over Dush Gibson's tired face. "You been pesterin', huh?" He swung his daughter up onto his shoulders.

Hooking her bare toes into the straps of her father's overalls, the girl jounced on his shoulders. "Play marbles, Daddy," she begged. "You show me."

"Althea," called her grandmother from the porch. "Don't you bother your daddy right now, he just worked all day. Help me feed the chickens."

Dush stopped under the oak tree, his smile widening. He reached up behind his head and grabbed his daughter. "So you think you can beat your daddy at marbles?" He swung her upside down. "You and who else?"

Althea laughed and kicked. "Jus' me. I'm

goin' lick you good!" Her father set her down, and she scampered around picking up acorns for the game. Dush Gibson took a stick and scratched a wide circle with a cross in the middle in the hard-packed dirt. A few of the chickens came closer to watch.

Dush motioned Althea to put the acorns in the circle. "Now, you and me each pick out one good big marble—acorn—for a shooter." He showed her how to set up the rest of the acorns inside the circle. "To shoot, we gotta stay outside the ring, see, and knuckle down."

Althea kept her eyes on her father and did just what he did. Kneeling outside the ring, she held her shooter between her thumb and forefinger.

"Now we take turns shooting acorns out of the ring, like this."

As the game began, cousins and uncles wandered down from the porch to watch. A short while later, Althea's grandmother, Lou

Gibson, came out of the cabin with a pan of mush. The chickens ran to her, clucking.

"Why, Althea," said her grandmother. "Look at you playin' good as the big kids." She whispered to her son, "Dush, honey, you ought to let that child win; she's tryin' so hard."

"Let her win?" Not taking his eyes off the game, Dush shot a cluster of three acorns out of the circle. "No, ma'am—she wouldn't learn nothin' if I let her win." He scooped the three acorns into his pile, aimed again, and shot the last one out. "Game's over. I won."

Althea's other relatives waited to see how the little girl would take that. Althea looked from her winnings, only four acorns, to her father's pile. She frowned, but she didn't cry. "Let's play again, Daddy. I'm goin' lick you good."

Dush Gibson didn't own the fields where he grew his cotton. Part of the time he worked for his father, Junius Gibson, on his farm. Part of the time he worked for his father-in-law, Charlie Washington. Charlie himself was a sharecropper—he farmed land owned by a white farmer. In exchange, he worked in the owner's fields part of the time. Usually the Gibsons could sell the cotton they grew and earn enough money to live on. But the last few years had been hard times.

One day after the cotton harvest in 1930, Dush Gibson hitched the mule to the wagon. He took his share of the cotton to town, a little town called Silver, to sell it. He came back singing:

> No use talkin', any man's beat
> With 'leven-cent cotton and
> forty-cent meat.

"You got eleven cents a pound for that cotton?" called Annie Gibson hopefully from the porch.

Swinging down from the wagon, Dush gave a short laugh. "I wasn't hardly thinking about what I was singing. No, ma'am, I didn't get no eleven cents a pound. They goin' to have to change that song to '*five*-cent cotton.'"

Annie came down from the porch, with Althea tagging behind. "Oh, my Lord. Only five cents a pound. And we didn't get but a bale and a half, what with the bad weather." She followed her husband to the pump near the cowshed.

"Third year in a row of bad weather," said Dush. He took off his straw hat. While his wife pumped the pump handle, he bent down and let the water run over his head.

Then Dush pumped more water into the trough for the mule. "Well, look at it this way," he said. "I could be out of work, like lots of folks."

"Yeah, you sure got work," said Annie. "You jus' ain't getting any *money* for working."

"Another good thing," Dush went on, "in town, at your daddy's store, they saying the bank in Manning went bust."

"How do you figure that's good, the bank went bust?" demanded Annie.

"Why, it's good—because we ain't got no money in the bank!" Dush started to laugh. Althea, looking up at her father, giggled.

Annie chuckled too. "There ain't nothing to laugh at," she said. But all three of them laughed and laughed.

A few weeks later no one was laughing. Althea's Aunt Blanche, one of Annie's sisters, had just died. Another sister, Aunt Sally Washington, came from New York City for the funeral. After the burial the adults stood around talking, looking strange in their best clothes. Althea and her baby sister, Millie, were scrubbed and dressed up too, and so were all the cousins. Althea's hair was braided so hard that it hurt her scalp.

Aunt Sally's clothes were much finer than the other ladies'. Dush Gibson told her, "You've got a nice sleek look to you, Miss Sally."

"I can't complain," Aunt Sally agreed. She had a good business, selling whiskey from her apartment. Under Prohibition, it was against the law to sell liquor in stores or bars. It was against the law to sell liquor from your home, too, but it was harder for the police to stop that.

Aunt Sally turned to Annie Gibson. "Sis, you and Dush better think about what I said. Come to New York."

"I don't know," said Annie slowly. "We've always lived in Clarendon County. At least here in Silver, we got a roof over our heads."

"But it's not our roof," Dush reminded her. "We don't own a darn thing. What if the crops fail next year too?"

"Come to New York," Aunt Sally urged again. "You all can stay with me till you get settled."

In the end, the Gibsons decided to leave Silver and move to New York City. First Aunt Sally would take Althea back with her. Then

Dush Gibson would make the long train trip from South Carolina to New York. Later, Annie Gibson would follow with little Millie.

Aunt Sally's home in New York City was as big as Junius Gibson's cabin in Silver, South Carolina. But Aunt Sally's was only one apartment in a big building full of apartments. Lots of other people lived in the building too.

When Althea stuck her head out Aunt Sally's window, she didn't see any rows and rows of cotton bushes. Instead she saw rows and rows of buildings along a paved street— not a dirt road. She didn't hear the chirping crickets and trilling mockingbirds of South Carolina, but the roar and rumble of cars. And instead of magnolia blossoms, she smelled the car exhaust.

Aunt Sally's kitchen had plenty of food, and Althea could eat all she wanted. Every night, when they got up from the dinner table, there was food *left over.* Not just corn mush and boiled greens, either. Aunt Sally could have pork chops or fried chicken every night of the week, if she wanted.

And the people! Back on the farm, Althea was used to seeing nobody but Gibsons and Washingtons for days on end. But New York City was full of strangers. It seemed that half of them came to Aunt Sally's apartment to buy whiskey. Lots of family folks came by Aunt Sally's, too. Sometimes one of the uncles would take Althea along on errands.

One of those first days, Althea walked along West 145th Street holding her Uncle Junie's hand. He had to pull her along to keep going. Her head swiveled back and forth, trying to see everything. A steady stream of people flowed along the sidewalk: men dressed in business suits, policemen with nightsticks in blue uniforms, workmen pushing handcarts. Here was a lady dressed so fine, finer than Sunday best, leading a fluffy little dog on a red leash. There was another lady up on a rooftop, hanging laundry on a clothesline.

Around the corner from Aunt Sally's building, Althea spotted a group of boys kneeling on the sidewalk. They drew a circle with chalk and put colored glass balls inside it. Althea tugged her uncle's hand. "Look what those boys doin', Uncle Junie. They's playing marbles, only with a bunch of pretty little balls."

Her uncle glanced at the boys, then stared down at her. "Why—what'd you think they play marbles with?"

"Acorns," answered Althea slowly. She was afraid Uncle Junie was going to laugh at her. It seemed everything was different in New York, even marbles.

Uncle Junie did laugh, but then he pointed to a store up the street. "Say, there's a five-and-dime. How'd you like to play with your own real marbles?"

Back at Aunt Sally's, Althea knelt on the

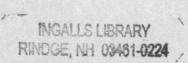

carpet and emptied her bag of marbles. She loved the way the shooter, the biggest marble, felt in her hand. It was heavy and smooth, perfectly round. She took aim and shot another marble, and they made a nice *clack*. Althea couldn't wait to play with Daddy when he got to New York.

Althea Is a Handful

Two months after Aunt Sally brought Althea to New York, Dush Gibson arrived at Aunt Sally's on West 145th Street in Harlem. Annie and the baby would come later, as soon as Dush could send his wife money for the train fare.

One afternoon Althea woke up from her nap very thirsty. From her bedroom she could hear voices in the parlor—Aunt Sally and her visitors. Althea thought she'd go to the kitchen and get herself something to drink without bothering her aunt. There'd be something nice in Aunt Sally's ice box: milk, or iced tea, or soda pop.

In the kitchen Althea found a large jug on the table. The liquid inside was golden brown, like iced tea. Althea picked up the jug—she was tall and strong for her age—and took a great big swig. No, that wasn't iced tea. She kept taking big gulps anyway.

Then Althea lost track. The next thing she knew, she was back on the bed. Aunt Sally and Daddy were holding her down while a doctor pumped out her stomach. Aunt Sally was moaning as if she was the one having her stomach pumped. Daddy shouted at her, "Don't you have no sense, leaving whiskey out so a child could get at it?" He shouted at Althea, too: "Don't you have no sense, chugging whiskey like it was iced tea?"

After things quieted down, Althea lay on the bed. She felt awful. Daddy and Aunt

Sally were talking in the kitchen. Dush Gibson asked, "What are we gonna do with that child?"

"That Althea, she's a handful," agreed Aunt Sally.

The trouble was, the grownups were too busy to watch Althea every minute. Dush had a job as a handyman in a garage. Aunt Sally had a job as a maid, and besides she had to tend to her whiskey business.

Althea's mother finally arrived from South Carolina. For a while after that, Althea couldn't get away with much. But during the next couple of years, Annie got busier and busier. Althea's brother, Daniel Jr., was born, and then little Annie.

Mrs. Gibson tried to get Althea to help look after the younger ones, but it seemed she needed more looking after than the three of them put together. Althea got into one scrape after another. She got used to hearing people say, "That Althea, she's a handful."

Every now and then, when Althea got to be too much for the New York family, her father would take her to Philadelphia. His sister Daisy Kelly lived there, where her husband worked as a Pullman porter on the train. Althea would stay with Aunt Daisy for a while, to give Annie and Dush a rest.

"Now you behave for Aunt Daisy, understand?" said Althea's father as he left to go back to New York.

Althea liked staying with Aunt Daisy. Aunt Daisy was a snappy dresser, and she loved to laugh. Althea's older cousin Pearl was nice. Also, the man next door to Aunt Daisy had a car of his own. He was always tinkering with it. Althea was proud to know someone who owned a car, and she liked to watch him work on it.

One Sunday morning Aunt Daisy said to

Althea, "I'm going to dress you up real nice for Sunday school. You're gonna feel like a whole new little girl when I get through with you."

Althea already liked the girl she was, but she was curious to see how Aunt Daisy would change her. So she stood patiently while her aunt braided her hair and dressed her in a frilly white dress and white stockings.

Finally, Aunt Daisy fastened a big white silk bow on her head. "Don't you look fine!" Aunt Daisy held up the hand mirror, and Althea smiled. Oh, she did look fine.

"Now, Pearl and me gonna fix ourselves up fine too," said Aunt Daisy. "You go play in the backyard till time for church. Just be careful to keep clean, you hear?"

"Yes, ma'am." Althea skipped out to the backyard. There wasn't anything interesting to do there. She'd like to climb the big tree, but she might get her pretty white dress dirty.

Hearing clanking and clinking from the street, Althea went around the house to the sidewalk. The neighbor man's car was parked at the curb, and his legs were sticking out from underneath it. Althea stooped down to talk to him. "Hi, mister. Want to see my Sunday dress?"

"Not right this minute, honey," he said. "I'm changing the oil."

"You working on your car?"

"Uh-huh."

The neighbor man wasn't going to pay her much attention this morning, Althea could see that. For a while she tried to watch him work. But even by squatting next to the car and craning her neck, she couldn't really see underneath the car. She'd have to lie under the car like the man, and of course that would get her white dress all dirty.

Standing up again, Althea noticed a big bucket on the sidewalk beside the car.

"Mister, I bet I could jump right over this bucket."

"Mm," said the man from under the car. He was doing something with his wrench.

"You don't really believe I could, do you? Look!" Althea jumped over the bucket, her white Mary Jane shoes just clearing the rim. "Did you see that?"

"Real nice, honey," he said absently. "You hush now. I gotta keep my mind on this oil pan."

"But you didn't look! Look, I'm doing it again. Whoo-ee!" Again Althea jumped over the bucket. Bucket-jumping was fun, even if the man wouldn't watch.

"Althea!" It was Aunt Daisy, calling out the window. "Where'd you get to? It's time to go to church."

Finally, here was someone to watch her. "Look what I can do, Aunt Daisy," Althea called back. She crouched to jump once

20

more, but now she was thinking too much about her aunt watching. The toe of one shoe hit the bucket. The bucket tipped over, pouring car grease onto the sidewalk. Althea slipped, stumbled—and sprawled. White dress, white stockings, white silk bow and all, she was lying in a puddle of car grease.

Aunt Daisy was pretty mad that morning. But the next day Althea heard her talking on the telephone to a friend. "And just when I was sucking in air to scream at that child, she says, 'Look what I can do!' and falls right splat in the grease." Aunt Daisy was laughing so that she shook all over. "'Look what I can do, Aunt Daisy,' she says! *Splat.* Oh, that Althea is a handful."

One day Aunt Daisy and Pearl got dressed up to go out again. They were going to some kind of party, and a friend was going to drive them there in a car. This time Aunt Daisy didn't try to dress Althea up. "Just Pearl and

me are going, honey," she said. "You're too little for this party. The cleaning lady will keep an eye on you while we're gone."

Althea couldn't believe it. "You're going to a *party*? In a *car*? You gotta take me—please, please, please!" Aunt Daisy shook her head.

"That's the meanest thing I ever heard!" Althea exclaimed.

Aunt Daisy only frowned and folded her arms. "I surely wouldn't take any girl that acted so wild. Just yesterday, didn't you grab yourself up a branch and beat on those boys from the next block?"

"Those boys were chasing me," protested Althea. But Aunt Daisy had made up her mind.

Calming down, the young girl started thinking. Maybe there was a way she could go along without Aunt Daisy knowing.

A little later the friend's car honked in front of the house. Althea, crouching behind a low wall, watched as Aunt Daisy and Pearl came down the front steps. They did look fine in their best hats and high-heeled shoes. Aunt Daisy was wearing her fur stole.

Althea waited until her aunt and cousin were settled inside the car, chatting with the driver. Then, still crouching, she scuttled to the car and climbed onto the running board. Just as the engine started, she grabbed the door handle. Whoo-ee! They were off.

Althea kept her head scrunched down below the car window the whole way. The car raced down the street and veered around corners. *What a blip!* she thought. This was even more fun than riding in a car the regular way.

When the car finally stopped in front of a house, Althea stepped off the running board. She smiled at Aunt Daisy, opening the car door. They'd have to let her come to the party now.

But Aunt Daisy didn't get out. She just sat there staring at Althea. Pearl, peering out of the backseat, screamed. "Oh, my Lord, Mama! She was on the running board the whole time!"

As it turned out, the party wasn't that much fun for Althea. Aunt Daisy was so upset they had to help her into the house and have her lie down on the sofa and put a cool cloth on her forehead. People kept arriving at the party, and each new person had to hear the story of what Althea had done and scold her all over again. "What if you fell off and got run over? What would your poor auntie tell your mama and daddy? Did you think of that?"

Althea tried to explain that she'd been perfectly safe, holding on tight to the car door handle. But they wouldn't listen. They shook their heads, and they said to each other, "That Althea is a handful."

Soon after that, word came from Harlem, the section of New York City where the Gibsons lived. The family had moved into their own apartment on West 143rd Street, between Lenox and Seventh Avenues. Althea came back and joined the Gibson family again.

But she was still a handful.

The Game of Street Life

Now Althea was seven years old, and she went to school every day. At least, she got dressed for school every morning, got her lunch money from Mama, and started out in the direction of Public School 136. There were some things Althea liked about school. She liked her best friend, Alma. She liked recess.

But she didn't like the classroom, with its rows of desks bolted to the floor. She didn't like sitting still and quiet at her desk. And she didn't like the teachers telling her what to do all day.

27

Luckily, Althea decided, she didn't have to go to school every day. The first few times she played hooky, she didn't know enough to stay away from policemen. Three days in a row a neighborhood police officer grabbed her and hauled her back to P.S. 136. The teacher spanked her right in front of the rest of the class. "This is what happens to bad little girls who play hooky!"

Not if they don't get caught, thought Althea. Playing hooky was just like any other game. The more she practiced, the better she'd get at it.

Althea got much better at dodging the police. But if she stayed out of school, the principal would tell her parents. Then her sister Millie chanted, "You're going to get it when Daddy comes home."

Daddy could spank good and hard, Althea had to admit. And she didn't like how everyone else in the house listened from the next room. "Everyone" included Mama, Millie and Daniel

Jr. and Annie, and now Mama's youngest sister, Aunt Hallie, and her dog, Ruth. Althea refused to cry, no matter how much it hurt.

One time, after a long, happy day of shooting baskets at the park, Althea began to think about how Daddy would whip her. He used a strap, and it *hurt*. Around dinnertime, instead of heading home to 143rd Street, Althea stopped at the police station on 135th Street. "I'm afraid," she whined to the officer at the desk. "Daddy's gonna whip me good."

The desk sergeant raised one eyebrow. "Is that right? If you was my kid and played hooky all the time, I'd do the same thing."

And Daddy did whip Althea again. "Your mama and I didn't bring you all the way north to New York for you to end up on the streets," he said grimly. "How you goin' learn anything if you don't go to school? You might as well be back in South Carolina, picking cotton at five cents a pound."

Althea's mother added, "Why can't you just

go to school nice and do what your teacher says?"

"Millie and Bubba don't get into any trouble at school," Aunt Hallie put in.

But Althea kept on skipping school. How could she stay inside on a beautiful spring day, a beautiful fall day, or even a chilly, overcast November day? It made much more sense to be at the park, shooting baskets.

Besides, if her parents wanted her to learn, there was plenty to learn on the street. For instance, Althea and her friend Alma got very good at snitching fruit. The grocery stores in New York displayed their apples and bananas and oranges outside the store in tempting piles. My, that fruit was pretty!

All you had to do was walk past the display, swinging your arms a little. You didn't look at the fruit, except out of the corner of your eye, and you didn't stop walking. You just let your fingers pick up an orange as if you had no idea what that hand was doing. As you kept on walking, you slipped the orange into your pocket. You didn't stop to eat it until you were around the corner, out of sight. That was the snitching game, and Althea was good at it.

One spring morning when Althea was about ten, she and Alma and a couple of other girls bopped along the sidewalk. They'd go to the park, but not just yet. They'd wait until almost noon, when the truant officer always went to lunch.

"I'm hungry," announced Althea. "I'm going to get me a nice big yam and roast it." Strolling past the vegetable stand, she lifted a yam and tucked it under her arm. She could almost smell it roasted, see the beads of brown syrup on its skin, taste the sweet, moist orange flesh. She started to run toward the vacant lot in the next block.

But as she passed the policeman on the corner, he grabbed her arm and jerked her to a stop. "Where you going so fast? What've you done now?"

Althea tried to hide the yam behind her back, but it was too late. The policeman glanced from the yam in her hand to the vegetable stand in front of the store, and he knew exactly what she'd done. Keeping a tight hold on her arm, he dragged her toward the nearby police call box. "I'm going to call the paddy wagon to come and get you."

"No, please!" screamed Althea. "Please, I'll never do it again! I'll be so good, I swear!"

Finally the policeman turned away from the call box. "Okay. I'm a nice guy, so I'm gonna give you a break." Still gripping Althea's arm, he pulled her back to the grocery store. "But put that yam back right where you got it."

Meekly Althea put the yam back and slunk off around the corner. Alma and the others were waiting for her in the vacant lot. "I bet you don't dare go back and snitch that same yam," said Alma.

"I bet I do dare," answered Althea. "You all

go get boxes for a fire—I'll get the yam." Sneaking around the block, she waited until the policeman moved on toward the next corner. A few minutes later she was back at the vacant lot, and her yam was on a spit over the flames. "Ain't you a blip, Althea!" exclaimed Alma. Althea grinned modestly. It was all a game.

At the beginning of the summer of 1938, everyone in Harlem was talking about Joe Louis. Joe Louis was the world heavyweight boxing champion—and he was African American. "The Brown Bomber," they called him.

Although Joe Louis was the world champion, he'd been defeated two years ago by Nazi Germany's champion boxer, Max Schmeling. Now a Louis-Schmeling rematch was scheduled for June 22 at Yankee Stadium. The Gibsons gathered at Aunt Sally's that evening, crowding around her radio to hear the live broadcast.

"Come on, Joe," said Dush Gibson as he turned the radio dial. "The Nazis say Schmeling beat you with his *superior intelligence.*"

"The Brown Bomber gonna give that Nazi a superior right to the jaw," said Uncle Junie.

"Did you hear, some reporter asked Joe if he was scared of this fight coming up?" asked another uncle. "Joe says, 'Yeah—I'm scared I'm gonna kill Schmeling.'"

"You all, hush!" said Aunt Sally. "I want to hear every single word." She turned up the volume, and the living room filled with the roar of the crowd at Yankee Stadium. Seventy thousand people there were watching to see if Joe Louis could defeat Max Schmeling, champion of the "master race." All across the United States, millions of Americans, black and white, crowded around their radios to listen to the fight.

The opening bell rang. The crowd in the stadium screamed, and so did the crowd around Aunt Sally's radio. Then they were all quiet. Althea leaned forward with the rest of them as the announcer described the fight.

Joe Louis was jabbing the German so fast, you could hardly see his glove move. Then a right to the jaw threw Schmeling against the ropes. Schmeling tried to come back, but Louis kept punching: another right to the jaw, a left and a right to the head, a left hook—and one last right to the jaw.

"And it's all over," said the announcer. He was shouting to be heard above the screaming crowd. "All over in two minutes, four seconds of the first round."

Althea, her family, and everyone else in Harlem poured out onto the streets. With a pie tin in one hand and a spoon in the other, she banged the tin and hollered. The city was one big party, with people honking horns and cheering and dancing through the streets. Someone started a chant, "Ain't you glad? Ain't you glad?"

Althea chanted too, beating the pie tin as she danced. "Ain't you glad?"

It was long after midnight when the Gibsons got back home to their apartment. In bed Althea thought about Joe Louis. She'd seen pictures of him in the newspaper with his gloved hands up in front of him, his eyes dead-calm focused on the other boxer. That Joe Louis, he was *somebody*. Althea thought, I want to be somebody too.

One morning that same summer, Althea came downstairs to meet her cousin Mattie. "Guess what, Al," the other girl greeted her. "They blocked off the street for us!"

Sure enough, there were sawhorses fencing off each end of the block. The city had done it so kids could play in the street, safe from traffic. Not only that—they'd chalked lines to mark a court and strung a net across the middle of the block.

With a whoop Althea scooped up the two

wooden paddles and ball beside the net. "Catch!" She tossed a paddle to Mattie, and they began swatting the sponge-rubber ball back and forth across the net.

Whap-bounce. *Whap*-bounce. This was fun.

Other neighborhood kids gathered to watch. Before long, though, they started nagging Althea and her cousin. "You're hogging the court. Come on, let someone else play."

"We aren't through yet," called Althea.

A few minutes later one of the neighborhood mothers stalked in front of the net and folded her arms. "The City of New York didn't make a 'play street' on 143rd for your private paddle tennis court, Althea. You take turns."

"Okay, okay." Althea hated to stop playing, but she knew she ought to be fair. "We'll play 'losers weepers.' Whoever wins can stay. But if you lose, someone else gets a turn."

A little later an adult play leader from the Police Athletic League (PAL) turned up and taught the kids the rules of paddle tennis. Playing real games was even more fun than messing around. Althea won game after game.

Up on the third floor, Millie Gibson watched from the window. "Mama, the PAL made a play street here just for Althea," she joked.

"It does seem like that," said Mrs. Gibson. "Or maybe they did it for me—at least I'll know where to find her now."

And so Althea spent that summer playing paddle tennis on the street in front of the Gibsons' apartment building. She loved the feeling of hitting the ball, leaning into a stroke so that it went just where she wanted it to, fast and hard. She especially loved returning the ball to the boy or girl on the other side of the net with a smash. *Whap*— the wooden paddle vibrated with the force.

The next summer, 1939, Althea played paddle tennis again. "Don't tell me you're gonna stay right here on this one little block while the World's Fair's going on," said Charles, one of her friends.

"How we gonna get there?" demanded Althea. "The fair's way the heck over at Flushing Meadows, in Queens."

"We could rent a bike," suggested Charles. "It's only thirty-five cents."

Althea didn't have thirty-five cents, and neither did Charles, and of course their parents couldn't spare that much money. Thirty-five cents at the grocery store would buy seven loaves of bread. But Althea and Charles knew how to get cash, and they started scrounging around in vacant lots, alleys, and trash barrels for deposit bottles. It was surprising how many people just threw their bottles away, instead of turning them in at the store and getting their money back. The deposit on a small Coke bottle was two cents, and a quart bottle got you a whole nickel.

A few days later Althea and Charles walked

into the bicycle store on 145th Street and poured their pennies and nickels onto the counter. They started out for Queens with Charles pedaling and Althea perched on the handlebars. Down Seventh Avenue they rolled to 125th Street, then across town on 125th to the East River and the Triborough Bridge. Here they switched off, and Althea pedaled across the bridge and through Astoria. Then Charles pedaled the rest of the way to Flushing Meadows.

Queens was flat. Long before they reached the World's Fair, Althea and Charles could see the white spike of the Trylon, the landmark of the fair. Before they reached the fence, they could also see the globe of the Perisphere. After a little investigation, Althea and Charles found a place to sneak through the fence without paying.

The World's Fair was like a city, a much bigger place than they could explore in one afternoon. But Althea and Charles tried.

They went through the Trylon and the Perisphere, gawking at the General Motors diorama of what the country was supposed to look like in the future. Everyone would have a car, it seemed, and they'd drive all over the country on smooth new highways.

In the RCA Pavilion, they saw an invention called a television. It was like a radio, except you could see the programs, not just hear them. There was a display of television sets in streamlined wooden cabinets, and a sign saying you could buy one in Macy's department store. Althea noticed the price for a set, six hundred dollars. She joked to Charles, "We better collect a few more Coke bottles."

All the buildings in the fair were new and clean, and the grounds were green with trees and grass. When Althea and Charles finally sat down to rest a moment, she remarked, "The World of Tomorrow doesn't look much like Harlem."

"Especially 143rd Street," agreed Charles.

Where they lived, the pavement was pocked with potholes and the buildings were grimy. There were no trees.

Althea thought something else, but she didn't say it out loud: Where were people like her and Charles in the World of Tomorrow? She hadn't seen one black person, or one poor person, in all these fine exhibits.

The Featherweight Champion of 143rd Street

By the end of the summer of 1939, Althea was the official champion of women's paddle tennis in New York City, even though she was only twelve years old. They had a ceremony to announce the award, and a news photographer took her picture with three smiling men, city officials. Althea was as tall as any of the men.

That week the picture was in the paper. Althea went around in a warm glow. Her mother cut out the picture and tacked it up over the refrigerator. People in the neighborhood called to her, "There goes the champ! Hey, Althea, I saw your picture in the paper!" Althea smiled and waved.

That fall, Althea started junior high school. Junior high was a different scene from elementary school. It seemed like half the girls were now crazy about boys, and the other half were mean and tough. Althea didn't want to be boy-crazy or mean. She just wanted to play basketball, go to the movies, and not bother with school too much.

One evening Althea was strolling down the street with a handful of pebbles. Thinking about the paddle tennis finals the past summer, she hauled off and hurled a pebble at a garbage can. *Clang!* Right on target. But a garbage can was too easy to hit. Althea aimed her second pebble at the stop sign across the street, and it rattled off the center of the O.

Just as Althea took aim at another garbage can—she'd hit the handle on the lid this time—she noticed someone swaggering toward her. Althea was tall for her age, but this girl was bigger and older.

"What, you supposed to be tough or something?" sneered the other girl. "You supposed to be *bad*?"

Althea shrugged. She didn't want to tangle with this kid. She crossed to the other side of the street. But the older girl crossed in front of her, blocking her way. "I guess you think you're hot stuff, getting your picture in the paper."

Althea knew it would be a mistake to run, but how could she get this tough girl to leave her alone? "No, I—*unhh!*"

The tough girl had punched her in the stomach, hard. Althea doubled up and dropped to her knees. She couldn't breathe—she was helpless. *Don't hit me again,* she begged silently.

The other girl looked down at Althea for a moment. "Guess you ain't as tough as you thought." Then she walked away, whistling.

When Althea got her breath back, she ran home and threw herself into her father's arms. "Daddy," she sobbed, "this mean ninth-grader beat me up for no reason at all!" She told him the story.

Dush Gibson hugged and patted Althea. But then he pushed her off to arm's length. "Listen here, kid. You let that girl get away with punching you, you might as well pin a sign on your back: HIT ME. Here's what you gotta do: You gotta go back out and find that girl. When you find her, whip her."

Althea couldn't believe it. She cried and begged, but her father only pointed to the door. "You don't go out and whip her good, *I'm* gonna whip the behind off of you."

Whip that mean ninth-grader? She'd get killed. Althea stomped out of the apartment. "You'll be sorry when I'm dead!" she shouted before she slammed the door.

A few minutes later Althea spotted the

tough girl leaning against a street lamp. Without a word she charged at her, punching that girl in the belly with all her might. As the ninth-grader doubled up, Althea punched her in the face. Punch in the belly—punch in the face. Belly, face. The bigger girl crumpled to the sidewalk, blood streaming from her nose.

"Don't you ever touch me again," said Althea. She walked away, rubbing her knuckles.

Back home, Dush Gibson laughed with delight. "I knew you could do it, champ! Ain't nobody gonna mess with you." He had Althea show him exactly how the second fight had gone. Then he worked with her, teaching her some moves that professional boxers used.

Every evening for weeks, Dush Gibson took Althea up to the roof to give her boxing lessons. Bubba came along, but Althea was the one their father worked with the most. "You're tall and strong, and you can hit," he

told her as they sparred. "Keep your hands up—block that punch. Move your feet— keep loose—that's the way." After a lesson one night, he said to Annie Gibson, "That Althea, she's not afraid of anything, and she's good. She's got the makings of a prizefighter. You know they have lady boxers now? It's not bad money, either."

"That's crazy talk, Dush," said his wife. "If Joe Louis or that new boxer Sugar Ray Robinson get cauliflower ears and a crooked nose, it doesn't matter. But Althea's a nice-looking girl, and I want her to stay that way."

Althea didn't really want to become a lady boxer, but she was glad she could take care of herself on the streets. There were some mean people besides that ninth-grader, and there were some street gangs. One of her buddies she played basketball with was the leader of a gang, the Sabres.

Althea and her friends were on the streets a lot, on their way to play basketball in the park. Sometimes if the weather was bad, or maybe even if it wasn't, they'd skip basketball and head for the Apollo Theater on 125th Street. The Apollo showed good movies, and on Fridays they had a big stage show.

The Apollo Theater held an Amateur Night once a week. Althea loved the professional musicians, but there was something especially exciting about seeing regular people step up to the microphone and sing. The amateurs didn't get paid, but they got the chance to perform for a big audience.

Some of these amateurs weren't much older than Althea and Alma. Ruth Brown, a singer who won first prize at an Amateur Night, was the same age as they were. She sang, "It Could Happen to You."

"I'm going to win some day," Althea told Alma.

"Sure you are," said Alma. She hummed a few bars of "It Could Happen to You," looking soulfully at Althea.

"I'm not kidding," said Althea. "I'll sing like that Ruth Brown, or maybe I'll play the saxophone."

"Play the saxophone?" Alma raised an eyebrow at her. "How you gonna win a contest playing the saxophone? You don't know how to play it. And you don't even have a saxophone!"

Althea laughed and shrugged. "I just like the sax, the way it sounds." Then she added, "You'll see."

Meanwhile Althea had to survive on the streets—and in school. If you wanted to stay out of trouble, school was worse than the streets sometimes. There was a girl in Althea's English class, for instance, who liked to pick on her. This girl, Lulu, sat right behind Althea. She'd wait until Althea was busy writing or reading, and then she'd give a good yank on her pigtails. "That's for skipping school yesterday, Althea," she whispered. "Naughty, naughty!"

Naturally Althea squawked. The teacher would frown, and the other kids giggled.

Then came the day when Althea decided not to be picked on any more. She turned around and fixed Lulu with a stare. "Leave me alone."

Lulu just grinned at her. A moment later she yanked Althea's pigtails even harder.

Finally, when the school bell rang for lunch, Althea turned to Lulu one more time. "If you're so bad, meet me after school today."

"Oh, I'm bad, all right," laughed Lulu.

"Yeah? We'll just see about that," said Althea.

The kids around them nudged each other excitedly. "Uh-huh! We gonna see!"

The word spread quickly through the school. Everyone liked to watch a fight, especially a fight between girls. When Althea walked onto the playground that afternoon, Lulu was waiting for her—and so was a crowd of other kids.

Althea and Lulu circled around each other, trading insults. "You're sure big, but so's a cow," Althea told her enemy. She shifted her feet, edging herself into a better position the way her father had showed her. "Cows can moo, but they can't fight."

"Who you calling a cow, pig-tailed pig?" said Lulu. She pushed out her chin.

"I say, cow," repeated Althea, crouching. "As in cow-ard." Without warning she brought her right fist up under Lulu's jaw, as hard as she could.

The crowd around the two girls gasped. One of Lulu's buddies tried to catch her, but the big girl slumped to the pavement. "She's out cold," whispered another of Lulu's friends. They backed away, looking from Lulu on the ground to Althea standing over her.

They're afraid of me, thought Althea. *Ain't that a blip!* She turned and walked away, feeling like Joe Louis or Sugar Ray Robinson. Feeling like somebody.

A Rich Folks' Game

It was a summer day in Harlem in 1940. On 143rd Street, the heat pulsed from the pavement. But hot weather didn't bother Althea. She was focused on playing paddle tennis, and as usual she was playing to win. She smashed serve after serve at her cousin Mattie. Mattie had some good tricks, but she just wasn't strong enough or quick enough to return Althea's serve.

In between shots, Althea was aware of a man on the sidelines watching the match. Without looking directly at him, she wasn't sure who he was. But she knew he wasn't one of the men out of work, sitting on a stoop on the shady side of the street, just filling in their time. She could tell by his alert posture that he was following the game.

Wrapping up the match with a last wicked serve, Althea turned her attention to the man and recognized him right away. "Oh, hi, Mr. Walker." Buddy Walker was a band leader and saxophone player. This summer he was working as a Police Athletic League play leader in his spare time. "I heard your band last week," said Althea. "You sure can play the sax!"

"Thanks, Althea," said Buddy Walker. "You sure can play paddle tennis. That's a deadly serve you've got there. Did you ever think about playing regular tennis?"

"Tennis? Naw." Althea smiled at the idea. "That's a rich folks' game."

Buddy smiled back. "Don't be so sure. I think you'd like it." He waved and strolled off.

But the next afternoon Buddy was back. He swung a wooden tennis racquet in each hand. "Come on, Althea. Let's go over to Morris Park and hit a few against the backboard."

At the park Buddy showed Althea how to hold the racquet, drop the ball at waist height, and swing to hit it. "As you swing, keep your eye on the ball, not the backboard . . . that's it. That's it."

After a couple of strokes, Althea got the rhythm of it. Again and again, she stroked the ball to the line on the backboard. It bounced back to her, and she hit it to the line again. Buddy was right—this was more fun than paddle tennis. With the racquet in her hand, she felt like a superhero with special powers.

Then Althea noticed that Buddy Walker wasn't talking anymore. She caught the ball and turned to him. "Is that what you meant, Mr. Walker?"

"Oh, yeah." He nodded. "Keep going."

After watching Althea at the backboard for half an hour or so, Buddy was almost jumping up and down with excitement. "I knew it! Listen, kid," he told Althea, "you could really make something of yourself." He talked fast, his eyes sparkling. "You don't want to spend the rest of your life hanging around the streets, wasting your talent, probably getting into six kinds of trouble. Tennis could be your chance to meet a better class of people."

Althea held up her hands, laughing, but she was excited, too. She agreed to meet Buddy at the Harlem River Tennis Courts a few days later. There on the public courts on 150th Street and Seventh Avenue, Althea played her first tennis match with one of Buddy's friends, while Buddy watched.

Buddy sure was right, thought Althea. There was a lot to like about regular tennis. On the deeper court, she could stretch out and take advantage of her long arms and legs. She could slam a volley into a back corner of the court, where the other player couldn't get to it in time.

Before long, Buddy wasn't the only one watching Althea. The onlookers around the courts drifted over to see this tall young girl play. Other players even stopped their own matches to watch her. She heard remarks: "Are you *sure* she's never played before?" and "Wow-ee! She aced that one!"

After the match, a man who belonged to the Cosmopolitan Tennis Club introduced himself to Buddy and Althea. Would Althea be willing to come to the Cosmopolitan and play a few sets with the tennis pro? He wanted other members to see what a natural talent she was.

Smiling, Buddy nodded at Althea. She nodded yes, dazzled.

Back home, the Gibsons were dazzled too. "They invited *you* to the Cosmopolitan?" exclaimed Millie. "That ritzy club on Sugar Hill?" She took a few steps with her nose in the air, holding one hand out limply, as if to show off diamond rings.

Althea pretended that Millie was being silly. But she did feel uncomfortable about going to Sugar Hill, the well-to-do neighborhood of Harlem. The distance from the Gibsons' apartment on 143rd Street to the Cosmopolitan Club on 149th Street and Convent Avenue was only about a mile. But as Althea walked up into the Sugar Hill district that first day, she began to feel very out of place.

Althea was used to the four-story brownstone buildings on 143rd Street. People in her neighborhood didn't go to private clubs—they sat out on their stoops to socialize. On Sugar Hill, though, you wouldn't catch anyone sitting out on the street. The apartment buildings were tall and dignified, with a uniformed doorman under each front awning. The sidewalks were clean, and there were no stray dogs on the streets. Althea thought the Sugar Hill doormen looked at her as if—well, as if she was the kind of girl who would steal a yam.

To her relief, Buddy Walker was waiting for her under the awning of the Cosmopolitan Club. He introduced her to Fred Johnson, the tennis pro, and Fred ushered her through the club to the clay-surfaced tennis courts. Fred had only one arm, which impressed Althea. If this man could make his living teaching tennis with only one arm, maybe she could hold her head up in a club full of rich folks.

Facing Fred across the net, with a tennis racquet in her hand, Althea felt her nervousness fade away. There was quite a group gathered on the bleachers to watch, but they weren't waiting for her to flash diamond rings. They wanted to see her play tennis. And Althea wanted to show them.

After Althea and Fred finished playing, the audience burst into applause. Fred beckoned her to the net and shook her hand. "Young lady, you made me work for every point. I wouldn't be surprised if they sponsored you to a junior membership here. I'll certainly recommend it."

Sure enough, the members of the Cosmopolitan Club did chip in to give Althea a membership. They loved the game of tennis, and they were proud of their club. They wanted to bring up the best young players, even ones who couldn't afford to belong.

The Cosmopolitan Club belonged to the American Tennis Association (ATA), a national organization of tennis clubs for African Americans. In the 1940s, black people were not allowed to join tennis clubs for whites or to play in the all-white United States Lawn Tennis Association (USLTA) tournaments. So African-American tennis players formed their own tennis clubs. And the clubs, through the ATA, held their own state and national tournaments.

For competitive black tennis players, this was better than no tournaments at all, but not exactly satisfactory. Like any competitive athletes, they wanted the chance to play against the best in the game. That was the way to improve, testing themselves against stronger opponents. By keeping African Americans out of major tennis competition, the white USLTA barred them from the top ranks of the game.

But for now Althea wasn't thinking about race problems in tennis. She concentrated on learning the game of tennis and beating everyone she played against. She started coming to the club several times a week, taking lessons from Fred Johnson and practicing. If the weather was good, they'd play on the clay courts of the Cosmopolitan Club. If it had just rained, they played on the asphalt Harlem River courts, which dried out faster. They could also play indoors, on wooden-floor courts, in the armory at 143rd Street and Fifth Avenue.

In a way this was a brand-new phase of Althea's life. But in a way it was more of what she already loved: playing ball games, getting better and better, working to win. Fred promised that when she was good enough, he'd enter her in an ATA tournament.

Sugar Hill Manners and Killer Strokes

Althea and Alma had spent another pleasant school day. After meeting in their homeroom class, they'd sneaked out of the building and spent the morning shooting baskets at the park. They ate lunch at a cheap restaurant, where you could fill up on collard greens and rice for thirty-five cents. To round out the school day (and keep out of sight of the truant officer), they went to a movie theater. Althea loved the movies just about as much as she loved playing basketball or tennis.

Today's movie was about a toreador, a bullfighter in Spain. When he first appeared and bowed to the crowd, Althea wasn't impressed. Bullfighting couldn't be much of a sport, she thought, if the toreador wore a brocaded costume and acted so polite. But then the bull—a huge, angry animal with sharp horns—trotted into the ring. Althea sat up straight. She kept her eyes fixed on the toreador as he swirled his cape, coaxing the bull to rush him. It was like an elegant dance, so deliberate and graceful—and inches away from death.

Now it was mid-afternoon, the time Althea and Alma would have gotten out of school—if they'd been in school. Althea waved goodbye to Alma and headed uptown. The movie was still in her mind as she walked to the Cosmopolitan Club.

In the ladies' locker room, Althea changed from her everyday skirt and blouse to shorts and sneakers. She said hi to the other girls and women in the locker room. Some of them smiled and greeted her, but some of them just gave her a cool look. All these people were the daughters and wives of doctors, ministers, lawyers, or prosperous businessmen. People who could afford to belong to the ritzy Cosmopolitan Club. No one else in this room was the daughter of a handyman in a garage.

"Good afternoon, Althea," said a cultured voice as Althea stepped out onto the courts.

"Hi, there, Mrs. Smith." Althea waved to a middle-aged woman in a spotless white tennis outfit. Mrs. Rhoda Smith had Sugar Hill money, people said, but she wasn't stuck-up like some members of the club.

"Althea." Rhoda Smith moved quickly but gracefully in front of Althea. "Say, 'Good afternoon, Mrs. Smith.'"

"Aw, for the love of—" Althea sighed. "How come you're always pickin' on me?" Mrs. Smith didn't budge. "Okay, okay. Good afternoon, Mrs. Smith."

Rhoda Smith smiled. "That's right. Doesn't

that sound much nicer than 'Hi, there'?" She straightened the collar of Althea's blouse. "Your tennis clothes could use a little bleach, dear. Tennis whites should be really white."

Althea was glad to go off to the backboard and practice strokes while she waited her turn for a lesson with Fred Johnson. Mrs. Smith had been awfully kind to her since the club took her in. And Althea knew that the wealthy woman had been one of the donors to her scholarship fund. People said Mrs. Smith had lost her only daughter, and it seemed like she'd taken Althea for a replacement daughter.

But why couldn't Mrs. Smith leave her alone about manners? The other day, as Althea and the society woman were playing doubles, a ball dropped into their court from another match. Annoyed, Althea swatted it out of her way. "Althea, dear," said Mrs. Smith. "In tennis, it is considered courteous to *return* a stray ball to its owners."

"But it was their fault, letting it come into our court," protested Althea. "Why do I have to be courteous about it?"

And the way Mrs. Smith said her tennis clothes should look—what was the point of bleaching, starching, and ironing tennis clothes, just to get them all sweated up? No point at all, in Althea's opinion. Unless you were a rich lady and wanted to keep your maid busy.

But later, while Althea was playing a practice set with the pro, she remembered a scene from the bullfighting movie. One of Fred's hard groundstrokes came right at her, and she stepped aside to let it go out of bounds. As the ball hummed past, an image of the toreador charged by the bull flashed in her mind. How gracefully his cape swirled as he stepped aside from the sharp horns! And yet, with all the bullfighter's elegant manners, he intended to kill the bull—if the bull didn't kill him first.

During her afternoons and weekends at the club, Althea spent almost as much time watching other players' matches as she did playing herself. Fred Johnson advised her to pay attention to this player's backhand, or that player's serve, or another player's footwork. Althea understood this. That's how you got good at any game, from basketball to boxing. You watched the good athletes, you thought, *I see how to do that*—and you did it. Pretty soon, if you were Althea Gibson, you could do it even better than the other players.

The trouble was, Althea wasn't that impressed with the tennis game of most of the ladies at the club. There was something too . . . *ladylike,* too held-back, about the way they played. Maybe they just weren't strong enough. Althea felt she learned more from watching the men.

The main thing she learned from watching women's matches was how to applaud politely. In the world of tennis, you weren't supposed to jump up and holler, "Sock it to 'em, sister!" at a good play. No, according to Mrs. Smith, you were supposed to keep your behind on the bench and just clap your hands. Maybe you could murmur, "Oh, nice point." Sheesh!

Almost all the people who played at the Cosmopolitan Club were African American. However, white players could enter American Tennis Association tournaments, if they qualified, and some of them did enter. Also, sometimes top white players appeared in exhibition matches hosted by the Cosmopolitan Club.

One day, at Fred Johnson's urging, Althea showed up at the club to watch Alice Marble play an exhibition match. Alice Marble had been a USLTA tennis champion in the 1930s and 1940s, winning the women's singles trophy in the national tournament at Forest Hills four times. She'd also won the singles trophy at Wimbledon, England, in 1939.

Still, Althea wasn't expecting too much, especially after she caught sight of Alice

Marble. She was a pretty blond woman. No wonder the snobs at the Cosmopolitan were so excited that she'd be willing to play here.

Then Alice Marble served. Stretching up as high as she could reach, she brought the racquet down on the ball with all her force. Althea's mouth dropped open. That wasn't any ladylike serve. That was a killer serve.

But Miss Marble didn't hang around the baseline, admiring her serve and waiting to see if her opponent would return it. Running up to the net, she put the ball away.

Applause broke out in the bleachers. Althea started to whoop, but caught herself and clapped hard instead. By the end of the match, her palms were sore from clapping. She thought, *Boy, would I like to play tennis like that!*

After the match Rhoda Smith joined Althea in the crowd around Alice Marble. "Now, dear, are you beginning to see what I mean?"

"I guess so, Mrs. Smith," said Althea slowly.

"You mean, the idea in tennis is to walk out on the court all dressed up in pretty white clothes, and be polite to everybody—and then play like a tiger. Beat the liver and lights out of the ball."

Rhoda Smith hid a smile with her hand. "Well, yes, that's one way to put it."

At Althea's next lesson with Fred Johnson, she pestered him to let her play in a tournament coming up. "Relax, young lady," Fred told her. "Keep practicing. When you're ready, I'll enter you in the New York State singles. Maybe next year."

Tournament Tennis and the SPCC

In the spring of 1942 the Cosmopolitan Club hosted the American Tennis Association New York State Open Championship. "*Now* you're ready," said Althea's coach, Fred Johnson. He entered her in the girls' singles. It was her first tournament, and she won.

As she accepted the trophy, Althea flashed a big smile around the audience. She saw sour looks on the faces of a few Cosmopolitan members. She knew why—they thought she was getting too cocky. Well, a winner had a right to be cocky, didn't she? Maybe a winner didn't have to pay so much attention to all Mrs. Smith's do's and don't's.

Soon afterward, Althea graduated from junior high school. Her parents weren't exactly proud of her. "I don't know how they even let you graduate, all the times you skipped school," scolded Mrs. Gibson.

Althea shrugged. She was just glad the school year was over, so she could concentrate on tennis. The ATA national tournament was at Lincoln University in Pennsylvania this summer, and the Cosmopolitan Club was paying her way. Most of the people at the club were nicer to her, Althea noticed, since she won the New York State tournament. People liked winners.

At the national tournament, Althea was sure she was going to win the girls' singles again. She watched the other girls practice, and none of them had as much power as she did. "I'll wipe them off the court," she told Fred Johnson.

Fred gave her a look. "Listen, Althea, it's good to be confident. But you should have more respect for your opponents. Nana Davis, for instance, is tougher than she looks."

"Who's this Nana Davis?" said Althea. By now other players were listening, but she didn't lower her voice. "Let me at her!"

As it turned out, Althea didn't play Nana Davis until the final round of matches. Althea and Nana had both won all their matches so far. Whichever girl won this match would receive the trophy.

By that time Althea had heard plenty of remarks about how poised and well-groomed the other girl was. "Not a hair out of place," people said admiringly. As Althea swung her racquet up for her first serve to Nana, she thought, *We'll see how your hairdo holds up when I'm through with you.* She came down on the ball with all her force.

Nana made a move to return the serve, but then pulled back. "Fault," the umpire called out. That meant that Althea's blistering serve wasn't any good. The ball had landed outside the service lines.

Determined to keep up the attack, Althea swung the racquet up for an even more blistering second serve. Nana Davis didn't even try to return this one, and for an instant Althea thought it was her point. But again the umpire called, "Fault." Nana had won the point—just by standing there and letting Althea make mistakes.

It was Nana's serve, and Althea waited with her knees bent and racquet ready. She planned to return the serve with a hard stroke to the back line. Then she'd follow up to the net and put the ball away before Nana had time to run forward. But there was a funny spin to Nana's serve, and Althea's return went out of bounds.

The match went on like that. Althea's serves and strokes were much harder and faster than Nana's, and she leaped around the court. Still, she kept losing. With every point Althea lost, she heard a boy in the stands laugh.

Why don't the officials throw him out? she wondered, gritting her teeth. I thought tennis was supposed to be so polite. Pretty soon Althea couldn't keep her mind on the game. All she could think of was killing that kid.

As for Nana, she just kept returning the ball, or letting it go out of bounds. *She was cool as a cucumber, point after point.* The match was over in two sets. Nana walked up to the net for the customary handshake, but Althea headed straight for the stands to find the laughing boy. "Where's that little jerk? *I'm* going to throw him out on his ear!"

Meanwhile, Nana Davis accepted the ATA national girls' singles trophy—still not a hair out of place.

Althea felt it wasn't fair somehow that she'd lost. But she didn't get much sympathy. "I hope you learned a lesson," said Fred. At the Cosmopolitan Club, some people seemed sorry that they'd sent her to the national tournament.

Well, tennis wasn't everything, thought Althea. She liked basketball just as much. She liked bowling, too, and she was really good at it. And what she'd really, really like to do was become a movie star. Or maybe a famous singer.

When the summer ended, it was time for Althea to start a new school, Yorkville Trade School. "I hope you're gonna buckle down and learn something in high school," said her mother.

"You're sure gonna show up at school every day," growled Dush Gibson, "or *I'll* teach you a lesson you won't forget."

It was worth a try, Althea supposed. At first she did go to classes most of the time. Sewing was actually kind of interesting, especially when her sewing machine broke down and she fixed it herself. But after a few months of Yorkville Trade School, she was bored again.

Life fell into a pattern: Althea would skip school for a day. The truant officer would call the Gibsons. That night Mr. Gibson would give Althea a whipping.

The next day Althea would disappear. She'd spend the whole day at a movie theater, watching the same double feature over and over. Or she'd sneak over to a friend's house. Some girls' parents didn't pay so much attention to whether they went to school or not.

At night Althea knew her father would be waiting for her, boiling mad. So she just didn't go home. She hopped on the subway and rode it downtown and into Brooklyn, all the way to New Lots Avenue. She rode it back uptown to the other end of the line, Van Cortlandt Park at 242nd Street. And she rode it back across Brooklyn again. There were some tough-looking characters on the

subway, but Althea could be tough too. If one of them looked at her funny, she gave him her don't-mess-with-me stare.

When Althea did come home, of course, she got it good. She couldn't tell Dush Gibson, "Don't mess with me." He beat her with a strap. "You know your mama's been walking the streets looking for you?" he shouted. "Is that what you're trying to do, keep your poor mama out on the streets of Harlem until two o'clock in the morning? Is it? Huh?"

Althea honestly wasn't trying to make her parents frantic about her. The solution, she decided, was to live somewhere else. Then they wouldn't know if she didn't go to school or didn't come home at night. Then they wouldn't worry.

Finally she heard about a place called the Society for the Prevention of Cruelty to Children. If you could convince them that your parents were really cruel, they'd let you live there. So Althea went down to the SPCC, on Fifth Avenue at 105th Street. "Look what my father did to me," she told the social worker. She pulled up her blouse to show the red welts on her back.

Althea felt a little guilty at the social worker's shocked expression. She didn't mean to give them a bad opinion of her father. He was just doing his job, trying to make her behave. But she was tired of being punished, even if it was her own fault.

The SPCC had to let Althea's parents know where she was, and her father came down to 105th Street to take her back home. But the SPCC let Althea choose, and she wanted to stay. She liked the girls' dormitory here. There were crisp clean sheets on the bed and good hot meals in the dining hall. This SPCC life was all right.

Althea didn't mention her new address to anyone at the Cosmopolitan Club, though. Mrs. Smith and the others were horrified enough when she didn't return a stray ball politely. They'd have a fit if they knew she wasn't even living at home.

After a few weeks at the SPCC, Althea decided they had too many rules and regulations. "I want to go back home now," she told the social worker.

The woman looked at Althea suspiciously. "Hmm. I thought you said your father was so mean, you never wanted to see him again." She paused, then added, "All right. But if you continue to have trouble at home, we'll have to send you to the girls' correction school in Hudson."

Uh-oh, thought Althea. She'd heard stories about the girls' "correction" school—it was like prison for kids. "Yes, ma'am," she said to the social worker. But she was determined to stay away from the SPCC from then on.

Mr. Gibson came down to 105th Street again to pick Althea up, and the SPCC released her into his custody. She was glad to be going home, although she was a little afraid of what her father would do to her. But on the subway ride uptown, she began to sense that something had changed. Her father didn't talk much, and he didn't have that steamed-up look like he was about to explode. His shoulders were slumped.

Back in the Gibsons' apartment, Althea's mother had a discouraged look to her too. "Now what're you going to do?" she asked Althea. "You ain't old enough to just stop going to school."

Althea certainly didn't want to go back to Yorkville Trade School. But it turned out she could get into a work-study program instead. The school system let her work at a job during the day as long as she went to night school in the evenings. Althea got a job as a waitress, and she was proud of making her own money and even paying a little rent to her parents.

As for night school, Althea stopped going

after a couple of weeks. Nobody from the school system checked up on her. Mr. and Mrs. Gibson knew that Althea wasn't going to classes, and at first they nagged her about it. But her father seemed to have given up on beating sense into his oldest daughter.

That suited Althea fine. She had a lot of interesting things to do with her evenings, like going to the bowling alley or shooting baskets with her friend Gloria Nightingale. Gloria and Althea played basketball in an industrial league on a team called the Mysterious Five. They wore red and white shorts and played to win.

Besides sports, there were movies—Althea never got tired of watching movies. And there was always something exciting going on at the Apollo Theater on 125th Street. On Wednesday nights, Amateur Night, young performers came from as far away as the South to try their luck. The winner got fifteen dollars and the right to perform at the

Apollo, with their big band, for a week. One night Althea got up and sang—and won second prize, ten dollars.

The school authorities never came after Althea for dropping her night classes, and she continued to work during the day. Most of the jobs she had were just a way to make a few bucks. Working as a counter girl in a coffee shop, or as a chicken cleaner in a butcher shop, was nothing exciting. But one job, at the New York School of Social Work, Althea really liked. She was in charge of sorting, delivering, and sending out all the mail. She knew that all the offices in the school were counting on her, and she did her work quickly and carefully.

One Thursday evening, when Althea had been a mail clerk for six months, she was at the bowling alley with her friends. Gloria started talking about plans for the next day. "Sarah Vaughan's at the Paramount Theatre," she said. "That sure is where *I'm* gonna be tomorrow!"

"Me, too," the others chimed in. It was settled—they'd all take the day off to go to Times Square and see Sarah Vaughan.

"I gotta work tomorrow," said Althea wistfully.

"Oh, come on," said Gloria. "Who's gonna care if you miss just one day? Tell your boss you're sick." She pretended to call on the telephone, coughing into the receiver. "Ma'am, I'm afraid I'm at—*hack, hack*—death's door."

The next afternoon Althea was leaning over the balcony rail of the Paramount with her friends. That Sarah Vaughan! Her voice soared so high it seemed like the top of your head would come off. It throbbed so low it made your toes curl. Listening to Sarah, you felt you'd lived through what the song was about. Althea sure was glad she hadn't missed this. She hadn't called in sick, but she'd tell her supervisor she'd been too sick to even pick up the phone.

Monday morning at the New York School

of Social Work, a secretary told Althea they wanted to see her in the office. Althea's heart sank. Standing in front of her supervisor's desk, she tried a smile. She took a breath to explain about getting sick.

But her supervisor didn't smile. "What happened to you on Friday?" Without waiting for an answer, she went on, "I had to sort and deliver all the mail myself, and it was late."

"I'm sorry," said Althea. She'd never felt so uncomfortable as she was under this woman's serious gaze. Althea really was sorry, and for some reason it seemed important not to lie, at least. "I—All my girlfriends were going to the Paramount to see Sarah Vaughan. I thought maybe it wouldn't be so bad—" She knew now that it *was* so bad. They had counted on her, and she'd let them down. "I won't do it again, I promise."

The supervisor hesitated, then shook her head. "I simply can't have somebody in that job who would leave it untended for such a foolish reason. I'll have to let you go and get somebody else."

Althea begged and pleaded, but that was the end of it. It reminded Althea of the ATA national tournament, when Nana Davis had won the finals. Just because Althea made stupid mistakes. It wasn't fair! This is what she got for being honest for once. Well, from now on she'd do whatever she felt like.

For the next couple of weeks, Althea didn't work or even show up at home. She heard her mother was looking for her, but she didn't care. She bummed around the streets, sleeping over with this friend or that. In a pinch she could always ride the subway all night.

Then late one morning, while Althea was sleeping on a friend's broken-down sofa, a knock at the door woke her up. There was no one else in the apartment, and the knocking wouldn't stop. Finally Althea stumbled to the door wrapped in a blanket.

Two stern-faced ladies were waiting for

her. "Althea Gibson? We're from the Welfare Department," said the shorter, stouter woman. "We're giving you one last chance before we send you up the river to the girls' reformatory."

Althea felt a chill, and not just from her bare feet on the cold floor. "Up the river" was the way people talked about Sing Sing, the prison on the Hudson River for dangerous criminals. Girls' reform school had to be almost as bad, and she'd do anything not to get sent there.

As it turned out, the Welfare Department just wanted her to live in a furnished room in a decent private home. She'd have to check in with Welfare once a week, so they could keep track of her. While she looked for a new job, they'd pay her an allowance.

"Ain't that a blip?" Althea crowed to her friends. "Everybody's happy!" The Welfare ladies were happy because they knew where Althea lived and because they thought she was trying to get a job. Mr. and Mrs. Gibson were happy too, because they figured the Welfare Department was looking after their wild daughter. Althea stopped in to see her family every now and then, and they had nice friendly visits without any shouting.

As for Althea, she was happiest of all. Once a week she showed up at the Welfare Office to pick up her allowance. Otherwise, she spent all her time playing tennis and basketball, or bowling with Gloria and the gang.

The Doctors Prescribe

During those years of Althea's struggles with her family, the schools, and the Welfare Department, she kept on showing up at the Cosmopolitan Club. She practiced, she took lessons from the club pro, and she tested her game against anyone who would play her. As a result, her tennis game improved steadily. In 1943 there wasn't any ATA national tournament, because the United States had entered the war with Japan and Germany. But in 1944 and 1945, Althea won the ATA girls' singles trophy.

In August 1945 Althea turned eighteen. Now she was completely free to do whatever she wanted. No one—her parents, the schools, the Welfare Department—could tell her where to live or how to spend her time. (Of course, her parents had given up trying to tell her anything a long time ago.) Althea got a job as a waitress and moved in with her friend Gloria's family.

One day that fall, at the bowling alley with Gloria, Althea noticed a familiar face two lanes over. Did she know that man? He had a trim, powerful build, and he moved as gracefully as a cat. The woman with him was exceptionally pretty. They both seemed to be in their twenties, and their clothes were casual but expensive-looking.

Althea paused with her fingers hooked in the bowling ball. "I know that guy," she remarked to Gloria, "but what's his name? Nah. I don't know him, but I know who he is. He's *somebody*. He's a dancer."

Gloria laughed. "Man, are you off base! Don't you know who that is? It's Sugar Ray Robinson!"

Althea laughed, too, and hit herself in the head as if to jog her brain. "No wonder he looks familiar! He's only in the papers every week for winning some fight." She'd heard radio announcers comment on how graceful the Sugar Man was.

"Not only that," said Gloria, "but I know Edna, his wife. Come on, I'll introduce you."

Althea felt shy about meeting someone so famous, but Sugar Ray and Edna were friendly. Althea quickly covered up her shyness by acting bold. "Mr. Robinson," she teased him, "maybe you're the champ in boxing, but I'm the champ in bowling. Want to play? I'll beat you good."

The pro boxer laughed and pointed at her. "I bet you just could—I watched you bowl that last string. By the way, call us Ray and Edna, honey."

The four of them began chatting about boxing and bowling, then moved on to baseball. Jackie Robinson, a talented African American, had just been signed to play on a white minor league team, the Montreal Royals. The girls told Sugar Ray and Edna about their basketball team, and Althea mentioned her wins in ATA tennis. Sugar Ray was surprised to hear that Althea had won the national ATA girls' singles trophy in 1944 and 1945. "You sure don't look like a society girl," he remarked.

Althea laughed. "Well, I'm not."

"But you sure move like an athlete."

Althea glowed. Coming from the Sugar Man, this was the highest praise. "Well, I am," she agreed. "Next summer I can enter the women's division of the ATA, and I'll win that, too."

That night after bowling, Sugar Ray and Edna invited the girls out for a bite to eat. Before long, Althea was good friends with the Robinsons. They took her along to their vacation spot out in the country, at Greenwood Lake. Sometimes they'd let her drive their fancy cars, although she didn't have a driver's license.

There was something Althea really, really wanted, but she'd never ask her own parents. They hardly had enough money to pay the rent. But she wanted so much to have a saxophone of her own to play. Listening to jazz, hearing the sax throb and wail, she'd fallen in love with it. It could express any feeling just like a human voice could, only with ten times the power.

Finally Althea got up her nerve to ask Sugar Ray if he'd pay for a secondhand sax. Sugar Ray said yes! Buddy Walker, since he was a sax player himself, helped Althea pick out the instrument at a pawnshop and bargain the price.

In 1946 Althea was now old enough to play in the women's division of the ATA tournaments.

From remarks she'd overheard, she knew the New York ATA had high hopes for her. There was a feeling of opportunity in the air for black athletes, now that Jackie Robinson was signed up to play in a white league. The ATA paid Althea's way to the national tournament in Ohio that summer.

During the tournament Althea won match after match. She felt like Wonder Woman, leaping around the court and smashing serves. By the time she reached the finals, she truly thought that no one could beat her. Her opponent, Roumania Peters, won the first set, 6-4, but Althea came back to win the second, 9-7.

The third set would decide the match, and Althea was sure she had more strength and stamina than the other woman. Why, look at the way Roumania was drooping around the court now. Althea was going to wipe her off the court without half trying.

But somehow Althea's exhausted opponent

managed to keep on returning her serves. Point after point, she kept the ball in play until Althea made a mistake. The final score for that set was Roumania 6, Althea 3. "Game, set—and match," called the announcer.

As Althea shook hands, she noticed that Roumania didn't seem tired at all. Althea had been tricked, and she felt like a fool. It seemed she had a lot to learn about tennis strategy.

Walking off the court, she comforted herself. It was no disgrace to lose in the finals, after all. She knew she'd played well, aside from getting overconfident and falling for Roumania's trick.

But while she was showering, Althea heard some talk that disturbed her. She recognized the voices of two women from the Cosmopolitan Club—women who didn't particularly like her. "I guess they've seen the light about *her* after that last match."

"Oh, yes," said the other. She gave a light,

sneering laugh. "I don't think New York will pay her way to any tournaments next year."

Outside the locker room a few minutes later, Althea noticed some of the New York ATA officials looking her way. Sure enough, they weren't smiling. They looked like they thought they'd wasted their money.

Althea sat down in the stands to watch the rest of the tournament. She felt suddenly hollow in the pit of her stomach. During the last five years, she'd come to take for granted all the help she was getting. She was so good, it seemed, she deserved to get her free ride on the tennis circuit. What if no one in the New York ATA—or even the Cosmopolitan Tennis Club—thought so any more?

Sunk in her gloomy thoughts, Althea didn't notice at first when two men sat down beside her.

"Hello, Althea. I'm Dr. Eaton," said the tall, slim man. She recognized him as one of the national ATA officials.

"And I'm Dr. Johnson." The other doctor was an ATA official, too. He was dark-skinned and handsome, with wavy hair. He shook her hand.

Althea couldn't imagine why they wanted to talk to her. Maybe they were going to tell her officially that her tennis days were over?

"We've been watching your game," said Dr. Johnson, "and we think you have real potential. But you're never going to live up to that potential the way you're going." He didn't seem to be criticizing or scolding her— just stating a fact. "Althea," he went on, "how would you like to go to college?"

"You could, you know," said Dr. Eaton. "There are plenty of scholarships available for young people like you."

"College?" Althea had to smile. "That would be great, except I never even been to high school."

The doctors stared at Althea for a moment, then exchanged glances. "I see," said Dr.

Johnson, rubbing his mustache. "Excuse us a moment."

During the next set Althea noticed Dr. Eaton and Dr. Johnson on the other side of the courts, deep in conversation with some other national ATA people. When they came back, they had a proposal that took Althea's breath away.

"Here's our plan," said Dr. Johnson. "You'll come to North Carolina and live with Dr. Eaton's family while you go to high school. In your spare time, Dr. Eaton will work on your tennis game with you—he has a private court."

"In the summers," Dr. Eaton went on, "you'll live with Dr. Johnson's family in Virginia. He'll coach you full-time and take you to the tournaments."

"All expenses paid, of course," said Dr. Johnson. "What do you say?"

Althea usually had a quick comeback in conversation. But now she looked from one man to the other with her mouth open. They'd just planned her whole life for the next several years. They wanted to make her a top-notch athlete, and they were willing to put their time and money into it.

"Think it over," said Dr. Eaton, handing her a business card. "Here's my address. Write me after you get back to New York."

At the tournament Althea had thought she'd have to say yes to the doctors. How could she turn down such a generous offer? But back in New York, she hesitated. This was a great life she had here, now that she was eighteen and free. How could she leave just when she had things the way she wanted them? How could she move from New York, the most exciting city in the country, to a Southern town?

Althea needed some good advice. Her parents couldn't help—all they knew about was sharecropping in South Carolina and barely getting by in Harlem. Friends like Gloria couldn't help either—the biggest decision they made was where to go out Saturday night. Althea had to talk her decision over with high-powered people with big ambitions.

So Althea went to Sugar Ray and Edna Robinson's. She took her saxophone, the one Sugar Ray had bought for her. They liked to play together, Sugar Ray on the drums and Althea on the saxophone, and the music would help her think.

"I can't go live in the South!" Althea wailed to Sugar Ray and Edna. She didn't remember Silver, South Carolina, which the Gibsons had left when Althea was only three. But she'd heard plenty about the way black people were treated in the South. Southerners had a whole unfair system known as "Jim Crow." Black people had to use separate drinking fountains and ride in the back of the bus. White people could beat black people up or even kill them, and get away scot-free.

"You know where Dr. Johnson lives?" she went on to Sugar Ray. "In Lynchburg! Can you believe any black person would live in a town called *Lynch*burg?"

"Listen, kid." The champion boxer pointed at her with a drumstick. "I know all about the South, 'cause I did most of my growing up in Georgia. It's real mean, all right. But you can't turn the doctors down just because you're scared."

Althea didn't like being called scared. "Okay, but how can I start high school all over again? It bored me crazy when I was only fourteen. How can I stand to go back now I'm nineteen?"

"No one says you're gonna *like* going back to high school at your age," said Sugar Ray.

"Althea, honey," Edna put in, "don't you see, this is your big break. When your big break comes along—for heaven's sake, grab it!"

"Amen, sister," said Sugar Ray to his wife. He went on to Althea, "You'll never amount to anything just bangin' around from one job to another like you been doing. No matter what you want to do, tennis or music"—he nodded at her saxophone—"or what, you'll be better at it if you get some education."

Her friends were right. The next morning Althea went to the dime store for an envelope and a piece of paper. She stood at the post office counter, writing her answer to Dr. Eaton. She wished she'd paid more attention in English class years ago, during the lesson on how to write a letter. Dr. Eaton was going to think she was ignorant.

Well, he already knew that! *Just go ahead and write it, girl,* Althea told herself. I'M COMING, she scrawled across the paper. THANK YOU VERY MUCH. Addressing the envelope to Dr. Hubert A. Eaton in Wilmington, North Carolina, she stuck a three-cent stamp on it. Her big break had come along, and she was grabbing it.

Hard Training

One hot September morning a couple of weeks later, Althea woke up on the train. She'd boarded the train yesterday at Pennsylvania Station in New York. She'd spent an uncomfortable night, lying across two seats in the coach car. Now they were in North Carolina, and the train was slowing down. "Next station stop, Wilmington," called the conductor.

Althea's eyelids felt like sandpaper. She'd dozed off and on through the night. Each time she woke up, she went through the same thought cycle. First she'd think, *This is it, my lucky break!*

Then her doubts would start pestering her:

How can I fit into the Eaton family and act the way Dr. and Mrs. Eaton expect me to? I didn't even want to mind the Daddy and Mama I grew up with, and they didn't expect much.

Is it really as bad as folks say in the South? If I'm walking on a sidewalk and a white person comes toward me, will I have to get off the sidewalk? Will I have to give up watching movies, because the movie theaters won't allow black people?

I can't give up movies!

But this is my big break.

The thoughts flapped in Althea's head like newspapers blowing around a vacant lot.

The train wheezed to a stop in Wilmington. Althea climbed off the train carrying her two cardboard suitcases. They were strapped with belts so they wouldn't fall apart. One suitcase held her tennis clothes, and the other held everything else. Her precious saxophone hung from her neck.

Althea looked for Dr. Eaton on the platform, but instead, a uniformed chauffeur came up to her. "Welcome to Wilmington, Miss Gibson." He picked up her suitcases.

On the ride to Dr. Eaton's house, Althea stared out the window at cotton fields. She felt so strange and mixed up. If Dush and Annie Gibson hadn't moved to New York sixteen years ago, she'd be out there picking cotton right now. On the other hand, if she'd turned down the doctors' offer and stayed in New York, she'd be looking forward to the matinee show at the Apollo Theater right now.

The car pulled into the driveway of a big classy house. Walking into the Eatons' kitchen, Althea was aware that her hair was sticking up from her head. She hadn't had a chance to really work on it before she got off the train. Also, she wondered if she should

have worn a dress for this special occasion. But she didn't even own a dress. She was wearing an old skirt and blouse, rumpled from her night in the coach car.

Mrs. Eaton beamed at Althea. "Welcome, dear." She gave her a big hug. "We've been looking forward to meeting you! How was your trip? Are you tired? Are you hungry? You just help yourself to anything you want—this is your home." She introduced Althea to the Eaton children and the maid.

Althea was hungry and was glad to fix herself some bacon and eggs. But she couldn't say she felt at home. *Me,* she thought, *living in a house with a maid?*

After breakfast Mrs. Eaton showed her the bedroom that was going to be hers. Althea could hardly believe she had a room to herself, let alone a nice one like this. The bed seemed *too* nice to sleep in. The sheets weren't just clean—they were starched and ironed smooth!

This new life didn't seem real. It took Althea the longest time to do everything that day. She was still putting away her things in her room when Dr. Eaton came home from the office. "Do you feel like hitting any?" he asked. "Or are you too tired?"

"Oh, no," said Althea. Her tiredness seemed to evaporate. A few minutes later she was in her tennis clothes and down on the court in the Eatons' backyard. "Service," she called, happily tossing a ball up to meet her racquet. *Now* she felt at home.

But then Althea went back to school. From her first day at Williston Industrial High School, she knew it would be even harder than she'd feared. Starting high school over again! groaned Althea to herself. *I should have just gone ahead and done it the first time, in New York. That would have been a lot easier than walking into this Southern school.*

The kids were much younger than she was, of course. All the girls seemed to have pretty clothes and hairdos. They stared at Althea, whispering behind their hands.

Althea thought she'd like singing in the school choir at least. But with her strong contralto voice, she didn't belong with the girl altos. The choir director asked Althea to move over and sing with the boy tenors, and she didn't mind. But the girls giggled about it so much that she got fed up and quit the choir.

The school was going to let Althea graduate in three years, if she could do the schoolwork. That was a big "if"! Althea knew she should really start over in the seventh grade, not the tenth. But she sure didn't want to spend more than three years in this school.

For the first few weeks she did everything right. She went to school every day. She studied hard. She was polite and helpful around the Eatons' house. She showed up for family meals.

Every afternoon and weekend Althea spent on the tennis court, practicing. Tennis was the only way she had to let off steam—that, and playing in the high school band. She thought the guys in the band were nice, especially the trumpet player.

But this rule-bound kind of life made Althea feel so pent up. Even the way people talked down South started to get on her nerves. Their words came out so . . . slowly . . . as if they had all the time in the world. Althea felt like snapping her fingers to hurry them along. She wanted to yell, "Just spit it out!"

One evening all the Eatons had gone out, and Althea was up in her room studying. Looking up from her books, she felt her good resolve giving way, like one of her flimsy cardboard suitcases. Outside the window she could see Dr. Eaton's mother's car. There it sat in the driveway, like it was inviting her to jump in and turn the key. Wouldn't the trumpet player be surprised if Althea showed up at his house on the other side of town? What a blip!

The trumpet player *was* surprised, and very glad to see Althea. They rode around town and had some laughs. Althea didn't go wild, though. Before it got too late, she dropped off her friend and raced back across town.

Whew! The Eatons were still out. Althea had noted how the front fender of Mrs. Eaton's car was lined up with a certain shrub. Now she parked the car in exactly the same spot.

But the next morning, when Dr. Eaton called Althea downstairs, she knew she was in trouble. Without saying good morning, he asked, "Did you take my mother's car out last night?"

Althea knew a friend of the doctor's must have seen her driving around. She didn't try to lie. "Yes, sir."

"You're aware that you don't have a license, aren't you?"

Althea was not that much shorter than Dr. Eaton, but this morning she felt very small. She couldn't look him in the eye. "I'm sorry, Doctor," she muttered. "I just thought I'd take a little spin and come right back."

The doctor didn't shout or strike out at her, but Althea knew he was as angry as her father had ever been. Too late, she realized that this was like the time she'd lost her job at the New York School of Social Work. Like the social work people, Dr. Eaton had taken a chance on her. He'd trusted her—and she'd thrown her chance away.

With her head still bowed, Althea heard Dr. Eaton take a deep breath. She waited for him to say he was putting her on the next train back to New York. Instead, he walked out of the room.

All that day Althea had plenty of time to think about how foolish she'd been. She thought about how the Eatons had welcomed her into their home. They'd given her a room

119

of her own—they'd even given her an allowance like the other Eaton kids.

As she made her bed, Althea thought about what it would be like to go back to sleeping on Gloria Nightingale's sofa in Harlem. She went out to the tennis court and practiced her strokes. She wondered, *Is this the last time I'll get to hit balls on this court?*

But Dr. Eaton never said anything more about what she'd done. As for Althea, she never broke his rules again. She studied twice as hard and practiced tennis even harder. The next weekend, Dr. Eaton invited a tennis player—a man—to play against her. The man beat her, but just barely.

At the end of the third set, Dr. Eaton held a towel out for Althea. He was beaming at her. He called to the other player, "Didn't I tell you?"

Dr. Eaton's really proud of me, Althea thought. *I'll never let him down again.*

The next time Althea felt like busting out,

she picked up her saxophone. She felt close to Sugar Ray and Buddy as she played all her favorite songs.

Meanwhile, up north in New York, times seemed to be slowly changing. In April 1947 Jackie Robinson played his first baseball game with the Brooklyn Dodgers on Ebbets Field. But down in North Carolina, segregation remained in full force.

Although Dr. Eaton was a fully qualified medical doctor, he couldn't practice at the local hospital. His African-American patients couldn't be treated there either. So like many black doctors of the time, he had his own clinic.

Likewise, Dr. Eaton opened his private tennis court to local black tennis players. African-American players weren't allowed on the public courts, so they came to the Eatons' backyard from miles around. So did some white players. Although these people could play on the public courts, they hated segregation. Althea heard one white tennis player, looking sad and ashamed, mutter, "No sense in it at all."

A Long-Range Plan

Althea's new school, Williston Industrial High School, didn't have a tennis team. At school she let out some of her athletic energy by practicing with the boys' football and baseball teams. She heard shocked comments from the girls: "Look at her throwin' that ball just like a man!" *That's the point, honey,* said Althea silently. She threw the ball harder than ever.

It was lonely for Althea Gibson. She was the only nineteen-year-old in her ninth grade classes, the only Northerner in a Southern high school, and the only serious female athlete. Thank goodness for the band!

Some of the band members belonged to a jazz combo, playing at places around town for a little money. Althea was delighted when they invited her to play the saxophone and sing with them. Those little girls in the school choir might giggle at her strong contralto voice, but the jazz group's audiences loved her.

In the summer of 1947 Althea went to Lynchburg, Virginia, to stay in Dr. Johnson's handsome three-story house. Like Dr. Eaton, Dr. Johnson had a tennis court in his backyard. A former varsity running back on the Lincoln University football team, Dr. J. was a tough coach. Because of his boundless energy, his nickname was "Whirlwind."

Althea was a high-energy person herself, but Dr. Johnson expected a lot of her. Every day was full-time tennis, from first thing in the morning until late at night and even in her dreams. Along with other players training for the ATA tournaments, Althea took lessons from Dr. Johnson, played games on his court, and practiced, practiced, practiced. Dr. Johnson had a machine, called a stroke developer, that shot balls across the net for a player to return. It was like playing an opponent who never got tired, and it built up Althea's strength and accuracy.

In July it was time to hit the road for the ATA tournaments. Dr. Johnson crammed several players into his Buick and drove them to Washington, Philadelphia, New York, New Jersey, and back down to Missouri and Kentucky. The Buick was big, but not really big enough for six athletes and all their luggage. Althea, at five feet eleven inches tall, was especially uncomfortable in the car.

After a long, hot road trip, they'd have to find a hotel where "Negroes" were allowed—always a second-rate hotel without air conditioning. Once they didn't even make it to the hotel. The Buick had a flat tire, and it was raining too hard to change. They spent that night in the Buick, sleeping in a pile like a litter of puppies.

That summer of 1947 was a hopeful time for African-American athletes. In their spare moments, they followed Jackie Robinson's first season with the Brooklyn Dodgers. Robinson had to face ballpark crowds who yelled insults or even sent him death threats. But right from his first game, he proved he could hit and run and field as well as any white player in the league.

In the ATA tournaments Althea competed in women's singles and also in mixed doubles events with Dr. Johnson. By the end of the summer she'd won all of her singles matches, and she and Dr. Johnson had won all but one of the doubles matches. Her tennis game was more consistent, more focused. The doctors' "medicine" was paying off.

For the final tournament, the ATA nationals,

Dr. Eaton joined Dr. Johnson's group. As Althea worked her way through the first round to the semifinals, he watched intently from the stands.

In the finals she faced her old enemy Nana Davis. Althea had an extra grudge against Nana now. Nana had been talking about her in the women's locker room, saying that Althea didn't know how to behave on the tennis court. She was spreading the story about their match in 1942, when Althea lost and then stormed off the court without shaking hands. "She was a crude creature," as Nana put it.

Looking at Nana across the tennis net, Althea could see that the other young woman hadn't changed. She was still perfectly groomed and poised. But Althea Gibson was no longer the "crude creature" who'd lost to Nana in 1942. She'd learned how to keep her eye on the ball and her mind on the game. Althea beat her in two sets, 6-3, 6-0. Althea Gibson, the new women's singles champion of the ATA, walked smiling to the net to shake hands with Nana.

The moment of triumph was exciting, but Althea felt let down when she read the notice in the *New York Times* the next day. A few lines at the bottom of a page, that's all it was worth to be the best woman player in African-American tennis. There was a much wider world of exciting tennis going on in the USLTA. But because of the color of her skin, Althea Gibson was shut out.

Next summer, 1948, Althea won the ATA women's singles championship again. That was nice, thought Althea later, as she sat watching the men's singles matches. But now she needed a bigger challenge. Playing in the ATA, Althea wasn't going to make much more progress in her tennis game.

I'd give my right arm to play those white girls, thought Althea. *Just let me at them!* Then she thought, *Although I wouldn't be much of a player without my right arm.*

As Althea laughed wryly to herself, Dr. Eaton sat down beside her in the stands. Something about the very casual expression on his face tipped her off: He was up to something.

"Althea," said the doctor, "how would you like to play at Forest Hills?"

Althea stared at him. "Huh! Who you kidding?" Forest Hills, New York, was where the all-white USLTA national championship tournament was played. This tournament was also known as the U.S. Nationals, the Nationals, the U.S. Championships, or the U.S. national championship tournament.

Whatever you called it, Forest Hills was where the best tennis players in America competed every year. It was for amateurs only, and there was no prize money, but winning at Forest Hills proved you were the best in the country. Of course Althea would *like* to play there.

Dr. Eaton looked into the distance with a

little secret smile. "It could happen."

By this time, Althea knew that Dr. Eaton and Dr. Johnson's strategy was even longer-term than she'd thought. The doctors had big plans. They wanted to help Althea, of course, but through her they also intended to help all black tennis players. Last year Jackie Robinson had broken the color line in major league baseball. Now Dr. Eaton and Dr. Johnson, and other black tennis players with money and influence, wanted Althea to break the color line in tennis. They wanted to open the USLTA—and world-class tennis—to African Americans.

What they needed was players so good that the white tennis world could be shamed into letting them play. The problem was, in order to become really good, even talented players have to challenge themselves against the toughest competitors. In 1947 an African American, Reginald Weir, had managed to enter a USLTA indoor tournament, but he hadn't done well.

In 1949, with the doctors and other supporters working behind the scenes, Althea got her first break from the USLTA. She was invited to enter the Eastern Indoor Championships in February. This tournament was held in her old neighborhood, on the wooden-floor courts of the armory at 143rd Street and Fifth Avenue.

Althea didn't win that tournament, but she got as far as the quarterfinals. More important, she'd shown the USLTA that she was worthy to compete with the best in the country. She was invited to go on to the National Indoor Championships the following week, in March. These matches were also held in New York, in the armory at 66th Street and Park Avenue.

Again, Althea got as far as the quarterfinals, where she faced Nancy Chaffee from

California. Althea was nervous, although it helped a little to see four African-American faces in the stands full of white faces. At least Ray and Edna Robinson, as well as the baseball hero Jackie Robinson and his wife Rachel, were rooting for her.

Althea lost that match, 6-2, 6-3. Still, she could see how much progress she was making in her game. And she was relieved and glad that most of the white players were friendly to her. Even Gussie Moran, the winner of the National Indoors, went out of her way to be nice to Althea in the locker room. At least it wasn't the tournament players themselves who wanted to keep her out of USLTA competition. Like Althea, they just wanted to compete against the best players, whoever they were.

A few months later, at the age of twenty-two, Althea graduated from high school. She was tenth in her class. In a way, she knew, this was more of an accomplishment for her than becoming a tennis champion. The big challenge hadn't been so much the schoolwork, but sticking out three years of high school with much younger kids. And three years of living in a small Southern town.

No white person in Wilmington had actually pushed Althea off the sidewalk, as she'd feared. But they did make her sit in the back of the bus. WHITE IN FRONT, COLORED IN REAR, read the sign just inside the bus door. As for the movies, Althea and her friends were allowed in the theater, but they had to sit in the back balcony, away from the white people. At the dime store, they were permitted to hand over money for a hot dog—but they couldn't sit there at the counter to eat it.

I hate this Jim Crow system, thought Althea over and over during her three years in Wilmington. *When I get out of school, I'm never going to live in the South.* Then she'd go out on Dr. Eaton's tennis court and smash serve after serve across the net, or she'd go on a gig with the jazz group and sing her heart out. For a while, she'd forget about living with Jim Crow.

Back in New York, Sugar Ray Robinson had a good idea of how hard it had been for Althea. He was proud of her for sticking it out. At graduation he sent her the money to buy her high school class ring. Althea's parents were glad she'd finally graduated, of course, but she didn't even think of asking them to buy her a ring. They were still barely scraping along.

In the summer of 1949 Althea won the ATA nationals for the third time. That fall she left for college. She'd won a full tennis scholarship to Florida Agricultural and Mechanical University in Tallahassee, Florida.

While Althea went off to college, Dr. Eaton and Dr. Johnson continued to work toward their goal. That winter they made sure Althea was invited to play in the Eastern Indoor tournament in February again. This time she won the final round in two sets, 6-3, 6-1. Clearly her game was even better than last year, and she was invited to the National Indoor Championships in New York again.

This year she fought her way as far as the finals, where she faced Nancy Chaffee again. Althea lost the final round in two sets, 6-2, 6-0, but she knew she'd done well to get that far. When she returned to Tallahassee, the whole college, including the marching band and the president, welcomed her back.

Now Althea was sure she'd proven herself as a national-class tennis player. The USLTA clubs would have to invite her to the regional grass court tournaments, wouldn't they?

It seemed that the answer was no.

The indoor tournaments were not so difficult to enter, because they were held in public places, like the armories. But the grass court tournaments, considered the real test of a tennis player's ability, were held in whites-only private clubs. Even in the North, private clubs could—and did—refuse to admit black players. Just this year, Dr. Ralph Bunche Jr., United Nations diplomat and winner of the Nobel Peace Prize, had been turned down by the West Side Tennis Club at Forest Hills.

If the USLTA clubs didn't give Althea a chance to play on grass courts, she wouldn't be able to prove she was ready for the national tournament at Forest Hills. So the white clubs at East Hampton, Long Island, and Newport, Rhode Island, tried to pretend that an enormously talented tennis player named Althea Gibson did not exist.

Breakthrough

Spring 1950 turned into summer. No USLTA tennis club invited Althea Gibson to play in a regional tournament. Then the July issue of *American Lawn Tennis* magazine came out, with a bombshell of an editorial by Alice Marble. Friends told Althea about it right away, but she couldn't believe it until she'd read the editorial herself.

Althea had admired Alice Marble, of course, ever since the time she saw the 1930s national tennis champion play at the Cosmopolitan Club. She'd never forget how

Alice Marble threw herself into her serve, or the way she leaped into the air to smash a return. But Althea was amazed that Alice Marble cared about Althea Gibson.

In this editorial Alice Marble laid out the facts as forcefully as she used to slam her serves into the opposite court: Althea Gibson had shown that she was a good enough player to compete in the USLTA regional tournaments. She might or might not be champion material—no one knew at this point. "But if she is refused a chance to succeed or to fail," Marble wrote, "then there is an uneradicable mark against a game to which I have devoted most of my life, and I would be bitterly ashamed."

In the same issue of *American Lawn Tennis,* there was an article titled "The Gibson Story" that backed up Alice Marble's passionate editorial. It included pictures of Althea serving a tennis ball, studying for her college courses, playing the saxophone, and as the runner-up in the National Indoor finals. Showing her as a real person, it seemed to suggest that it was only fair to give her a chance. The article quoted one sports columnist as saying that Althea showed "that she can be a fine player indeed if she is given the chance to develop naturally." That was a tactful way of saying, if racism in the USLTA clubs doesn't prevent her from competing against the best players.

Encouraged, Althea applied to enter the USLTA New Jersey State Championship tournament at the Maplewood Country Club. They turned her down. "Not enough information" was the explanation. It was the same old excuse—the USLTA clubs wouldn't allow Althea to play in their tournaments because she hadn't played in any of them before! "Sanctimonious hypocrites," Alice Marble had called them. That was a polite way of putting it.

But then an even more important tournament did accept Althea's application. The

Orange Lawn Tennis Club in South Orange, New Jersey, invited her to play in the Eastern Grass Court Championships. This was her breakthrough chance.

At the tournament in South Orange, Althea made it only to the second round of matches before she was beaten. This wasn't an exciting showing, but it wasn't bad, either. Then she played in the National Clay Court Championships in Chicago, and there she reached the quarterfinals.

In these two events, Althea proved that she could compete on a national level. Even the USLTA officials had to admit that. Tennis was a sport that prided itself on fair play, and they could no longer pretend it was fair to shut out such a well-qualified player. The USLTA gave in, inviting her to enter the U.S. Nationals. The president of the USLTA announced that Miss Gibson had been "accepted on her ability."

"That's all I ask," said Althea when she

heard the news. At the end of the summer, she was on her way to the West Side Tennis Club in Forest Hills.

Althea's old friends at the Cosmopolitan Club in Harlem were proud of her, and proud of their part in launching her tennis career. Rhoda Smith, who'd taken Althea under her wing and tried to teach the wild teenager some manners, was especially eager to help her now. She invited Althea to stay at her house on 154th Street during the national tournament.

Althea accepted gratefully. If she'd had to stay with her family in the crowded, noisy 143rd Street apartment, or sleep on her old friend Gloria's sofa, she couldn't be rested and ready for her first match. Althea knew it would calm her nerves about the tournament if she had a chance to visit the West Side Tennis Club beforehand. She asked Sarah Palfrey Cooke, a former national women's champion and a friend of Alice Marble, to give her a tour.

Sarah gladly took Althea out to Forest Hills. She showed her around the imposing Tudor-style clubhouse and the stadium, which had stone eagles on the corners of its roof. Sarah also played some practice games on the West Side Tennis Club courts with Althea.

The first day of the tournament, Rhoda Smith made sure that Althea ate a good breakfast of bacon and eggs, toast and milk. Rhoda also rode the subway to Forest Hills with her that morning of August 28, 1950. Althea had just turned 23.

Althea's trip from Harlem to Forest Hills had taken only half an hour—and yet it had also taken several years. *It's really me, playing at the West Side Tennis Club,* thought Althea as she walked up to the registration table on the front lawn. These grounds had been designed by Frederick Law Olmsted, the famous landscape architect who designed

Central Park. It was a good thing Sarah had showed Althea around. Otherwise, she'd feel as nervous as when she was a twelve-year-old street kid, walking up to the Cosmopolitan Club for the first time.

In the locker room Althea changed into her white flannel shorts, short-sleeved white shirt, and white socks and tennis shoes. She was grateful that Rhoda was there to protect her. The locker room was crowded with all the reporters and photographers who wanted pictures and quotes from her. Althea would rather not think about the fact that she was such big news.

But Alice Marble was there too, with some heartening words for Althea. "Have courage. Remember, you're just like all the rest of us." Althea put on the white warm-up sweater that a friend in the ATA had knitted for her, and she walked out to Court 14 for her first match.

Court 14 was the one farthest from the clubhouse. Some sportswriters took this as a further insult to the first black tennis player to compete in the Nationals, but Althea brushed that idea away. After all, the featured player nearest the clubhouse was a glamorous movie star, Ginger Rogers. Ginger Rogers might not be such a hot tennis player, but Althea personally would have been thrilled to watch her play.

Anyway, Althea was just as glad not to be the main attraction for the moment. It was bad enough that news photographers kept taking her picture with flash bulbs during her first match. Still, Althea won that match, 6-2, 6-2. Alice Marble was in the stands, clapping for every point. At the end of the match, Marble congratulated Althea and walked beside her to the clubhouse.

The next day Althea faced a much tougher opponent, Louise Brough. Brough had just won the British Open Championship at Wimbledon for the third time, and in 1947 she'd won the Nationals at Forest Hills. She was a strong woman with an attack style of playing and a fierce serve.

The Brough-Gibson match was played on the court in front of the grandstand, with every seat taken. Althea couldn't help being nervous. She lost the first set, 6-1.

Althea wished the crowd would just let them play tennis. As she put it later, "The only white thing I want to think about is the tennis ball." (Tennis balls were white, not yellow or orange, in those days.) But she couldn't help hearing a heckler in the stands. "Beat the nigger! Beat the nigger!" he shouted. What had happened to the refined manners of the game of tennis? Althea wondered.

In the second set Althea settled down. She aimed her big serve more accurately, and she didn't hesitate so much in returning the ball. She won that set 6-3. She noticed that Louise Brough looked tense, too. After all, as the champion, Louise had more to lose than the challenger.

The third set would decide the match. Althea and Louise Brough fought each other for every point, but finally Althea was ahead, 7-6. If she won the next game, she would win the match.

But then a sudden thunderstorm swept over the club. Rain drenched the courts, stopping all play. Lightning flashed, and a bolt struck one of the stone eagles on the corners of the stadium, toppling it.

The end of the Brough-Gibson match had to be postponed until the next day. Meanwhile, Althea read the reports in the evening newspapers. They said she was making history. She just wanted to play tennis!

Rhoda Smith patted Althea on the back and tried to calm her down. "Even if you lose tomorrow, honey, it won't make a particle of difference. You did yourself proud already." Somehow those words made Althea even more nervous.

By the next day Althea was a bundle of

nerves. As the Brough-Gibson match continued, Althea did get in one of her "ace" serves,
and she did rush the net for a kill shot on
another point. But Louise Brough won the
third set, 9-7—and Althea lost the match.

It was disappointing for Althea, to have her
chances ruined by bad weather and nerves.
But the ATA wasn't disappointed in her. They
urged her to plan on playing at Wimbledon
next spring.

Wimbledon! Forest Hills was the top tournament in the United States, but Wimbledon
was the most prestigious tournament in the
whole world. It was every tennis player's
dream to compete on the grass courts at
Wimbledon, maybe with royalty watching.

The USLTA wasn't quite willing to pay for
Althea's trip to England, but they wanted her
to make a good showing in the tournament.
They arranged for her to prepare for
Wimbledon by taking lessons from a top ten-
nis teacher in Detroit.

Detroit was the home of Joe Louis, champion boxer of the 1930s. When he heard Althea was coming to the city, he arranged to put her up in his own luxury hotel suite. One morning he took her to breakfast. Althea was thrilled just to meet the Brown Bomber, and she was deeply grateful for his encouragement.

Joe seemed to know just what it was like when people expected you to be a champion for your race. "Back in the thirties, when I was coming up, I went to church one Sunday. The reverend preached a personal sermon at me! He said God gave certain people gifts, and my gift was fighting, so I was supposed to uplift the spirit of my race. I was supposed to make the whole world know that Negro people were strong, fair, and decent." Joe rolled his eyes. "*Whew!* Anything else, Reverend?"

Althea laughed with relief. That was exactly the way she felt—she just wanted to play tennis.

Still, she couldn't help being touched when African-American groups in Detroit raised money for her expenses in England. And Joe Louis himself paid for her round-trip ticket.

Thousands of black people, famous and not so famous, were proud of what Althea Gibson had accomplished. As she carried her tennis racquets onto the plane to England, she knew that many, many hopes were flying with her.

The Biggest Disappointment

During the next few years, Althea was a disappointment to herself and many other people. She did not do well at Wimbledon in 1951. While her ranking in the USLTA climbed from ninth in 1952 to seventh in 1953, in 1954 she was ranked only thirteenth.

Althea did win the women's championship of the ATA every year, but that wasn't any challenge. It didn't seem like she was getting anywhere. *Jet,* a magazine for African Americans, ran an article about her titled, "The Biggest Disappointment in Tennis."

In her personal life, at least, Althea had made a happy connection. In 1951 she began spending a lot of time with Rosemary Darben and her family. Althea knew Rosemary from the ATA, where Rosemary was a good player, although not in Althea's class.

When Althea played in the Eastern Grass Court Championships in East Orange, New Jersey, she needed a place to stay. The Darben family lived in nearby Montclair, New Jersey, convenient to the tournament, and Rosemary was happy to share her room with Althea. Before long Mrs. Darben and her big, friendly family had more or less adopted Althea, and the Darbens' was her home whenever she was in the New York area.

Part of the reason Althea didn't progress faster in the early 1950s was that championship tennis is a full-time job. But in the 1950s, it was a job that didn't earn any money. USLTA tournaments were open only to amateurs, athletes who didn't get paid for playing in tennis competitions. USLTA players weren't allowed to endorse products or make money through tennis in any way.

Since Althea had to earn her own living, she couldn't afford to play tennis full-time. In those days there was no prize money to be won in women's tennis, even for champions. After Althea graduated from Florida A&M College in 1953, she had to find a job. She began teaching in the physical education department of Lincoln University in Jefferson, Missouri.

Although Althea was glad to have this job, she wasn't so glad to be living in the South. In May 1954 the U.S. Supreme Court had ruled that segregation was unconstitutional. But the ruling didn't seem to change everyday life at first. In Jefferson, Althea couldn't even find a bowling alley near campus to take her students to. The nearby bowling alleys were for whites only.

Besides the racism, Jefferson was a boring

town for someone used to New York City. Althea was glad to escape and go to tennis tournaments, especially around New York. With every visit to the Darbens she settled in further, sharing Rosemary's room and calling Mrs. Darben "Mom." One of the boys in the family, Will Darben, started dating her.

Meanwhile, she had a new coach, Sydney Llewellen. He taught tennis in Harlem and drove a cab for a living. Althea had known him for several years, and Sydney had been watching her career closely. When her tennis game seemed stalled in the early 1950s, he offered to give her lessons whenever she came to New York. He knew that Althea still had a lot to learn about playing tennis, and he thought he could teach her what she needed to know.

The first thing Sydney did was to change Althea's grip. Her first coach, Fred Johnson, had taught her the Continental grip. With this grip, the player holds the racquet the same way for either forehand or backhand strokes. That grip worked well for Fred Johnson, who had only one arm, but not as well for Althea.

Sydney also got Althea to make her stroke more flexible, and he worked her hard on strategy. "You've got the big serve, you've got the power stroke, and you know to rush the net," he told her. "That's all good, but it won't make you a champ. Know what makes champs? Champs are champs because—they win more points than they lose."

Althea, bouncing a ball with her racquet, gave him a disgusted look. "That's it? That's your pearl of wisdom?"

Sydney stared back calmly. "Think about it. When you played Maureen Connolly in 1951, did she win because she had a bigger serve? Because she hit a lot of fancy shots?"

"No," said Althea. She paused, remembering how Little Mo, the USLTA champion of 1951, had just kept returning the ball to her.

No matter how hard and fast Althea served and stroked, Maureen got the ball back over the net. She placed it exactly where she wanted it and let Althea make the errors. Maureen had won that match easily.

"Okay, you see what I mean," said Sydney. "We already know you're big and strong and fast. So I want you to work on hitting the ball accurately and consistently, point after point." He brought a big basket of tennis balls onto the court. Althea practiced serving, hitting ground strokes, and working the net, hour after hour, day after day.

Meanwhile, though, Althea was getting restless. Her salary at Lincoln University was meager, and she couldn't see much of a future for herself in tennis. During her two years in Jefferson, Missouri, she'd fallen in love with an army officer. He thought Althea was officer material herself, and he tried to talk her into joining the Women's Army Corps. She could make a better living as a

WAC, and she might be able to stay with the captain.

In the end, the captain and Althea broke up. He was much too old for her, she had to admit. But her other reasons to join the army still made sense.

In June of 1955 Althea went back to Harlem and told Sydney that she'd applied to the WAC. He couldn't believe it. "Are you nuts or something? You're giving up tennis, after you got this far? You know what you're saying? You're saying you want to throw away your chance at the best tennis career since Helen Wills!"

"Syd, that's ridiculous," said Althea. Helen Wills was a tennis legend of the 1920s, and she'd won the USLTA Nationals three times as a teenager. "For one thing, I'm almost twenty-eight. If I was any good, I'd be the champ by now. For another thing, I want to earn my own way. People have been giving me lessons and plane tickets and buying me clothes and racquets ever since I was a kid, and what did they get for it? I know the ATA is fed up with me. Well, I'm fed up with tennis."

Syd couldn't talk Althea out of applying to the army, but he did convince her to sign up for the USLTA Nationals at Forest Hills again. She didn't think anything would come of it, but she figured she owed her coach that much.

In the USLTA tournament at the end of that summer, Althea lost in the third round. That was that, thought Althea as she showered afterward. This would be her last USLTA National. Soon the army would call her up, and that would be the end of her tennis career.

Althea sat down in the clubhouse of the West Side Tennis Club. She was thinking about how hard she'd worked to get here when Renville McMann, president of the club, joined her at the table. "Congratulations on a fine match today," he said. Althea thanked him, but she wondered why McMann, a big wheel in the USLTA, wanted to talk to her.

Renville McMann explained that the U.S. State Department had asked him to talk to her. They were going to send a national tennis team, two men and two women, on a goodwill tour of Southeast Asia. They particularly wanted Althea Gibson to be part of the team.

Southeast Asia, all expenses paid! Althea jumped at the chance. This was much more exciting than joining the army. And she didn't have to give up tennis yet. Also, of course, it was a great honor to be chosen for the U.S.-sponsored tour.

Althea figured that the State Department must have picked her because she was the top African-American woman tennis player. The United States was anxious to improve its image with other countries right then, when an ugly side of America had been in the news. That summer a fourteen-year-old African-American boy, Emmett Till, had been murdered in Mississippi for whistling at a white woman. The year before, the U.S. Supreme Court had ruled that racial segregation was unconstitutional, but public schools in the Deep South still refused to admit black children.

Althea was even happier about the tour when she learned that the other woman tennis player would be Karol Fageros. Althea had met Karol a few years ago, when Althea started playing in USLTA tournaments. It was impossible not to like Karol, a warm, sweet person—even if she did look like a movie star. Karol's nickname was the Golden Goddess.

A few weeks later the American team flew from New York to London, then to Rangoon, Burma (now called Myanmar). They traveled all over Southeast Asia—India, Thailand, Indonesia, Malaysia, Ceylon (now Sri Lanka), and Pakistan, playing in tournaments and exhibition games. Rooming together on the tour, Althea and Karol became good friends. They got along well with the two American men on the tour, too. Althea loved it all—feasting on exotic food, sight-seeing, trying on beautiful clothes, being honored at lavish parties.

The tour was a great adventure for all four of the Americans. But Althea, as a person of color, felt especially welcomed and appreciated in Southeast Asia. This experience was just the opposite of the shame she'd felt in the segregated South. Here the audiences applauded loudest for her, and children gazed at her as if she were a superhero. This treatment did something wonderful for her spirits.

The welcoming atmosphere didn't hurt Althea's tennis game, either. In tournament after tournament, she was the winner. Syd Llewellyn's training finally paid off, and she

played with steady concentration. When the tour ended in Ceylon in January 1956, Althea Gibson was the women's champion of Southeast Asia.

By now she had changed her mind about quitting tennis. During the Indian Championships in New Delhi, she'd met Angela Buxton, a player on the British team, and they hit it off. Angela urged Althea to try her luck in the European tournaments.

Full of new energy and hope, Althea traveled on to tennis tournaments in Germany, Italy, and France, as well as Egypt. She made a good showing overall, but the most important event before Wimbledon was the French Championships in Paris.

Althea had heard from Sugar Ray Robinson, who'd traveled in Europe, how wonderful Paris was. But for Althea, sight-seeing by herself, the city didn't seem like such a big deal. She badly missed Karol, who had flown back to the United States after the Southeast

Asia tour. Althea was glad to meet Angela Buxton again, and glad to accept Angela's suggestion to be doubles partners.

The French Championships was one of the four Grand Slam tournaments, the major events in the tennis world. The three other Grand Slam tournaments were Wimbledon, the USLTA Nationals (now the U.S. Open), and the Australian Championships. If a player won all four tournaments in one season, he or she was said to have won a Grand Slam.

Angela Buxton, ranked No. 4 in England, was matched against Althea in the women's singles semifinals. During the match Althea's brassiere strap broke. It was a humiliating moment, with thousands of onlookers, some of them hooting at her, knowing what had happened. Not only that, but she had to leave the court to fix the strap.

Technically, leaving the court meant that she'd conceded the match to her opponent.

The officials wanted to give the match to Angela Buxton, but Buxton insisted on playing it out when Althea returned. Althea was impressed with Buxton's sportsmanship, especially since the result was that Althea won the match.

Now the stakes were very high. If Althea won her next match, she would be the first African American to win one of the Grand Slam tournaments. On May 20, 1956, Althea Gibson faced Angela Mortimer of England in the final match of the French Championships.

Althea won the first set, 6-3. But Mortimer fought back hard in the second set, and the pressure got to Althea. When she made a double fault and lost her serve, she also lost her temper and slammed the ball into the stands. Luckily none of the spectators was hurt, but Althea knew she'd committed a serious breach of tennis etiquette. But then she pulled herself together and won her next service. Game, set, and match went to Althea—and so did the French Championships women's singles trophy.

Since leaving the United States for Southeast Asia, Althea had won *seventeen* tournaments. She was definitely getting that championship feeling. On to England!

Before Wimbledon, Althea played several more matches in England. By now, she'd played more tournaments in a row than any other female player in the world. This year Althea felt she had a chance of winning Wimbledon. Many other people thought so, too, and Althea was favored 2-1 to win.

But in the quarterfinals at Wimbledon, Althea lost to American Shirley Fry. Like Maureen Connolly, Fry played with relentless concentration. Althea had already beaten her in a minor tournament, and at first it looked as if she would win this match too. But in the end, Shirley Fry beat Althea.

Afterward Shirley praised Althea's game and suggested that she'd lost only because of nerves. Althea herself said she'd lost because she tried too hard. One British sportswriter was sure that the audience for the Gibson-Fry match had a "tight-lipped, cold" attitude toward Althea, and that had drained the fighting spirit from her. The most likely explanation is that Althea had played in too many tournaments without a rest. She'd finally run out of her impressive stamina.

Angela Buxton made it to the Wimbledon finals, and Althea rooted for her friend as she played Shirley Fry for the championship. But it was Fry's year to win the women's singles trophy, a round gold tray called a salver. Althea and Angela consoled each other by winning the women's doubles trophy.

The Girl from Harlem and the Queen of England

In September 1956, a few months after Wimbledon, the tennis tour brought Althea Gibson and her rivals back to the USLTA nationals at Forest Hills. In the meantime, Althea had lost to Shirley Fry again at the National Clay Courts Championship in Chicago. Still, she hoped to beat her this time.

Althea, now twenty-nine, played well at Forest Hills, and she fought her way to the final round without losing a single set. Sure enough, Shirley Fry was the other finalist. In this Gibson-Fry match Althea put up a fierce battle, but she made too many mistakes. Fry, on the other hand, stayed calm and simply returned the ball from the baseline again and again. In two sets Fry won the match, 6-3, 6-4.

Althea was bitterly disappointed, but she wasn't crushed. "I'll beat her next time," she muttered on her way to the locker room. Althea knew how much her game had improved. In the last two years she'd moved from the thirteenth to the second spot in the world of women's tennis. Althea smiled at a description, in *Sports Illustrated* magazine, of her tennis style: "She moves rangily around the court like a slightly awkward panther." *Grrr,* she said to herself. *Watch out for the panther.*

Althea went on to the Pacific Southwest Championships tournament, where she was delighted to meet many of the movie stars she'd admired on the screen. She won that tournament, and at a celebration party afterward she was honored by the famous singer Nat "King" Cole.

Althea flew on to the Pan-American tournament in Mexico City, where she faced Darlene Hard in the finals. In the U.S. Nationals, Althea had beaten Hard in the quarterfinals, and now she beat her again. She barely had a chance to catch her breath before flying on to Australia. The Australian Lawn Tennis Association (ALTA) had invited her and Shirley Fry, all expenses paid. Althea and Shirley were to play in all the ALTA tournaments and some exhibition games as well.

Althea won two of the four biggest Australian tournaments, but Shirley Fry won the national championships. Althea was frustrated, because she was still losing points to Shirley on errors. Why couldn't she be more consistent? When Althea was on her game, she could overpower Shirley with her ace serves and sizzling groundstrokes. In one of their Australian matches, Althea won, 6-2, 6-4, in spite of the fact that a tennis ball hit her in the eye just before the match.

By the end of the Australian tour Althea and Shirley had become good friends. Althea was delighted for Shirley when she fell in love and decided to stay in Australia. Althea also knew this might be an opening for her. Shirley Fry, ranked No. 1 in women's tennis, was leaving the competition. If Althea didn't step into the No. 1 place now, it would be her own fault.

Next June, 1957, the USLTA paid Althea Gibson's expenses to Wimbledon. Three old friends saw her off from the New York airport: her coach, Sydney Llewellyn; Buddy Walker, who'd discovered her playing paddle tennis on 143rd Street years ago; and Sugar Ray Robinson's wife, Edna. Althea had a good feeling about this trip before she even climbed onto the plane.

Althea was now almost thirty, getting on in years for a tennis player. But she'd learned some important lessons in the six years since her first appearance at Wimbledon. For one thing, she now knew that you could set your-self up to win or lose before you ever stepped onto the court. This year, Althea didn't wear herself out in the weeks before Wimbledon. She played (and won) in three English tour-naments, just enough to warm her up for the big event.

In London Althea stayed with Angela Buxton, who had an apartment in the West End. Angela couldn't play in the tournament this year, because she'd sprained her wrist, but she was glad to support her friend. She helped Althea shop for a gown to wear to the Wimbledon Ball.

Althea had such a good feeling about Wimbledon this year that she had her win-ner's speech all prepared. She knew many people thought she was arrogant, and often she acted arrogant because she was insecure. But this time her confidence felt right.

Out at Wimbledon Althea won her first-round match, then her second-round match.

Now she was a finalist, and she and Darlene Hard from California would face off the next day. Althea had beaten Darlene Hard in the quarterfinals of the U.S. Nationals and in the finals of the Pan-American tournament last year. Still, that didn't mean beating her now would be easy. Obviously Darlene was playing well, or she wouldn't have gotten to the Wimbledon finals.

The night before the final match, Althea took especially good care of herself. Two friends from her ATA days had come to London to see Wimbledon, and she went out for a steak dinner with them. For Althea, who now spent so much of her time in the white tennis world, it was wonderfully relaxing to be with African-American friends on this particular night.

Back at Angela's apartment, Althea took a long, hot bath and then went to bed early. The next morning, July 6, Althea drove from London to Wimbledon with her two ATA friends in her rented car. In the clubhouse she changed into her white tennis shirt and pleated shorts.

In the locker room everyone was talking about Queen Elizabeth, who had never attended Wimbledon before. This year the Queen would be watching the finals from the royal box. That news might have made Althea nervous, but instead it made her feel excited and glad. It seemed like another sign that this day was Althea Gibson Day.

The weather at Wimbledon was sweltering hot. By 1:15, the time of Althea's match, the temperature was 96 degrees Fahrenheit, without a breeze. But the heat didn't bother Althea. In fact, steamy weather seemed to limber up her muscles, and her aim was more confident in the still air.

Althea and Darlene walked onto the court, making the traditional curtsy to the Queen. Althea had seen many movies in which women curtsied to royalty, so she felt confident about that, too. Althea won the toss for first serve and began serving hard and fast. She won the first set, 6-3, in twenty-five minutes.

It seemed that nothing could stop Althea now. On the other side of the net, Darlene Hard made error after error. Althea saw her opponent nod helplessly after each point. Althea knew how it felt to lose, but she would have no sympathy for Darlene until the match was over. She won the second set even more quickly, 6-2. The match was over, and Althea Gibson had won the most prestigious tennis tournament in the world.

"At last! At last!" shouted Althea, running up to the net. Happily she shook Darlene's hand, and they walked to the trophy table. While the two players waited, a red carpet was rolled out from the royal box to the table for the Queen to walk on.

Queen Elizabeth II, wearing a flowered dress, white hat, and white gloves, shook

hands with Althea Gibson, the girl from Harlem. The Queen's smile was warm. "My congratulations," she said. "It must have been terribly hot out there."

"Yes, Your Majesty," answered Althea, "but I hope it wasn't as hot in your box. At least I was able to stir up a breeze." She took the trophy, the golden salver, that the Queen held out. On the tray were engraved the names of all the previous champions. Now the name "Althea Gibson" would join the champions of past years. Filled with joy, Althea curtsied again and backed away from the royal presence—again, just the way she'd seen it done in movies.

In the dressing room Althea found telegrams of congratulations from Sugar Ray and Edna Robinson, from the principal of Williston Industrial High School in Wilmington, North Carolina; from Averell Harriman, governor of New York State, and many others. She couldn't read them all now. It was time to go back to Angela's apartment and get ready for the Wimbledon Ball.

Later, as Althea stepped out of the taxi in front of the hotel where the ball was being held, the waiting crowd applauded her. She wore the glamorous gown she'd bought and a pearl choker. At the dinner, she sat at the head table between the Duke of Devonshire and the men's singles champion of Wimbledon, Australian Lew Hoad. When it was time for Althea to give her speech, she thanked Buddy Walker, Dr. Eaton and Dr. Johnson, Fred Johnson and Sydney Llewellyn, Angela Buxton, and all the tennis opponents who'd challenged her to play her best.

Then the dancing began, led off by Althea and Lew Hoad. Later Althea was begged to sing for the party, so she went up to the mike. She sang "If I Loved You" and "Around the World." The audience applauded enthusiastically. Althea was on top of the world.

A few days later she flew back from London

to New York. To her amazement, a big crowd was waiting for her at the airport. There were reporters, photographers, and other media people, as well as New York City officials. Althea ignored them all and ran up to her mother. "I always knew Althea could do it," said Mrs. Gibson with tears in her eyes. Remembering times her mother had been in despair over her, Althea felt deeply satisfied.

After a celebration breakfast at the home of Bertram Baker, executive secretary of the ATA, Althea rode up to 143rd Street. Now she triumphantly bore a golden salver from Wimbledon. But she remembered so well the days of playing hooky, when her "trophy" was a stolen muskmelon under her jacket. It seemed impossible that Althea Gibson then, a street kid headed for reform school and worse, was connected with Althea Gibson now, the tennis champion of the world.

When Althea reached her old home on West 143rd, her father was leaning out the third-floor window. "You made it!" he hollered down to her. "I knew you'd get to the top!"

Althea looked around at the old neighborhood. The brownstone apartment buildings were still shabby, and the people pouring out to greet her were still poor. But their faces were shining with pride for her, the kid from Harlem who made good. Althea felt a lump in her throat. This welcome meant more to her than the letter of congratulations she'd received from President Eisenhower.

The next day the City of New York gave Althea Gibson a ticker-tape parade up Broadway from the tip of Manhattan. Flags flew from the buildings. Althea sat on the backseat of a convertible, wearing an orchid corsage and draped with ticker tape, smiling and waving. At City Hall, Mayor Robert Wagner presented her with the medallion of the city. Then there was a luncheon in her honor at the ritzy Waldorf-Astoria Hotel.

Ain't this a blip? thought Althea. She was

in glory. She deserved it, and she relished every minute. Althea Gibson had become "somebody."

But shortly after the celebration in New York, Althea got back to business. She had her sights set on the next challenge: becoming the women's tennis champion of the United States.

"I Couldn't Eat Trophies"

Althea Gibson had come a long way since her first USLTA national championship tournament. In August 1957, she entered the nationals once more. Instead of staying in Harlem and riding the subway to Forest Hills, she stayed at the Vanderbilt Hotel on Park Avenue. The hotel provided a car and driver to take Althea and the other tennis players out to the West Side Tennis Club each day.

In 1950 Louise Brough had beaten Althea in the second round of matches. This year, Althea met Louise again in the finals on

September 8. Louise was a former national champion, as well as a winner for four years at Wimbledon. But now she was past her prime. Althea won in two sets, 6-3, 6-2. She walked up in front of the marquee to accept her trophy from Vice President Richard Nixon. The trophy, a tall silver vase, was filled with red roses and white gladioli.

Althea had learned, in her years of tournament tennis, not to count on support from the audience. She'd played in front of crowds who shouted racial insults. She'd also played in front of crowds who sat silently hoping she'd lose. But today at Forest Hills, the applause burst over her in wave after wave. This was even sweeter than her victory before the Queen at Wimbledon.

That night, Althea threw a big party at the Vanderbilt Hotel for her family and friends.

During the next year Althea seemed to be riding high. The press voted her Woman

Athlete of the Year. Her picture was on the cover of *Time* magazine. She was the No. 1 player, worldwide, in women's tennis.

But even as she followed the tournaments from California to South America, from New York to London, Althea worried about earning money. On tour she was given a living allowance, but it didn't really cover all the little expenses like taxi rides and phone calls. A sporting goods company had hired her as a consultant, but that brought in only $75 a month.

After all these years of taking room and board, train and plane tickets, tennis lessons, sports equipment, and all kinds of gifts from other people, Althea longed to pay her own way. More than that, she wanted to do wonderful things for other people. It made her feel especially bad that she was living high on the tennis circuit, while her parents and brother and sisters were still stuck in that crummy apartment on 143rd Street.

June came around again, and Althea was off to England for the 1958 Wimbledon tournament. Now she was the one defending her title, proving that she really was the champion. She and her coach, Sydney, had decided she'd stick to the way she played best: Serve hard and run to the net.

This year, Althea faced Angela Mortimer in the finals. Althea had beaten Angela two years ago for the French championship, but now she got off to a slow start. Angela was on the point of winning the first set.

Then the "You're going to win" pep talk that Sydney had drilled into Althea's mind took over. "You're the champ," his voice seemed to speak in her head, "you can take chances, you can hit all-out on every shot." Althea let go with a mighty forehand stroke, driving the ball deep into Angela's backhand corner. The ball was just barely on the line— and the point went to Althea.

That was the turning point of the match.

Althea won the first set, 8-6, and then she finished Angela off fairly easily in the second set, 6-2. Althea Gibson was indeed the champion, and she had another golden salver to prove it.

In her spare time after her first championship year, Althea had written a book, *I Always Wanted to Be Somebody.* It was the story of her life, from sharecroppers' daughter to world tennis champion. She gratefully gave credit to all the people who had supported and encouraged and taken a chance on her. She dedicated the book to "my two doctors"—Dr. Eaton and Dr. Johnson, of course.

But she also complained that some African Americans wanted her to be a champion for her race. "I'm a tennis player, not a Negro tennis player," she said. "I want my success to speak for itself as an advertisement for my race."

Althea felt she should just be left alone to

play tennis, but that wasn't possible. Even as she'd played her winning match at Forest Hills for the U.S. championship in September 1957, a fierce struggle for racial equality raged in Little Rock, Arkansas. Governor Orval Faubus ordered the National Guard to block African-American students from entering Central High School in Little Rock. President Dwight Eisenhower responded by sending paratroopers to Little Rock to protect the black students. Racial issues were in the national headlines every day, and so it mattered that the new tennis champion was African American.

In September 1958, Althea returned to Forest Hills to defend her title as U.S. champion. This year, her challenger in the finals was Darlene Hard. Althea had beaten her fairly easily in the finals at Wimbledon the year before, but now Darlene won the first set, 6-3. Then Althea pulled herself together and steamrollered Darlene in the next two sets, 6-1, 6-2.

At the age of 31, Althea Gibson was on top of the tennis world, no question. Winning two years in a row at Wimbledon and two years in a row at Forest Hills proved that. No one would have been surprised if she'd stayed at the top of women's tennis for the next few years.

But she had already decided to drop out of amateur tennis. As she was leaving the West Side Tennis Club with her second USLTA nationals trophy, she spoke to a crowd of shocked reporters. "I wish to announce my retirement from the ranks of amateur tennis players."

The whole tennis world was stunned at Althea's news, but she explained that it was a simple matter of money. Trophies looked nice in a row on the mantel, but "I couldn't eat trophies," as she put it. The USLTA and the major tennis associations in other countries, such as England and France, still looked down on professional tennis players and did not allow them to compete. If Althea wanted to remain the amateur champion, she wasn't allowed to make money playing tennis.

How would Althea Gibson earn a living, then? She hadn't made firm plans, but she knew she was talented in more than one direction. She had tremendous energy. After her big success in tennis, she had confidence that she could do just about anything she set her mind to.

If Althea had been a white tennis champion, she could have made a decent living as a professional by endorsing sporting goods. Or she could have worked as a pro at a country club, giving lessons. But in 1958, what club would hire her? Private clubs wouldn't risk it—they knew that some of their members would be offended to take lessons from a black woman. Likewise, most sponsors wouldn't want her appearing in their advertisements. They didn't believe that promotion by an African American—even a world champion African American—would help their sales.

So Althea was hoping for a career outside the tennis world. Singing, for instance. She'd had this dream ever since she was a teenager, skipping school to enjoy shows at the Apollo Theater. Hadn't she won second prize in an Amateur Night in 1943? And now she was constantly asked to sing at parties and dinners.

Even before her second win at Wimbledon, Althea had been working at launching a pop singing career. She took voice lessons. She appeared twice on the enormously popular Ed Sullivan TV variety show, singing pop songs. In the spring of 1958 Dot Records released an album, *Althea Gibson Sings*.

Althea was also thinking of going into professional golf, where the prizes in women's tournaments were larger than in tennis. Althea hadn't played that much golf, but she really liked the game. She knew she had a killer swing. She was just a natural-born athlete, so why couldn't she become a golf champion too?

But the next opportunity that turned up for Althea wasn't in singing or golf, or any kind of sports. Now, in 1959, director John Ford offered her a part in his new film. Not only that—the main roles would be played by the big-time stars William Holden and John Wayne. Ever since she was a young girl, Althea had been crazy about movies, and she jumped at the chance to be in one.

The movie, *Horse Soldiers,* was set in Mississippi during the Civil War. Althea's role wasn't glamorous—she played the maid of the Southern belle. Still, she was thrilled to hobnob with Hollywood stars and see moviemaking from the inside. She also hoped the movie appearance would help her singing career. Her album hadn't sold well at all, but she hadn't given up on singing.

Nothing further came of Althea's movie

appearance, either in the way of another movie role or invitations to perform as a singer. And no record companies were interested in making another Althea Gibson album.

In 1960 Althea finally got a job that allowed her to make money by playing tennis. The Harlem Globetrotters, a black professional basketball team, asked her to tour the United States with them. She and another woman would play exhibition tennis matches to open the Globetrotters' basketball games. Audiences loved the Globetrotters, and the pay would be good.

Althea asked Karol Fageros, her roommate and friend on the 1955 Southeast Asia tour, to join her on the Globetrotters tour. Karol wasn't quite in Althea's class as a tennis player, but the two made a good contrast on the court. Entertainment was the idea of the exhibition matches, and Karol, "the Golden Goddess," was known for her blond good looks.

Althea enjoyed her tour with the Harlem Globetrotters in 1960, and she was delighted to have some real money at last. She bought herself a fast new car and a beautiful apartment in New York. Even more satisfying, she bought her family a ten-room house, big enough for her brother and sisters as well as her parents. It was in the suburbs on Long Island, away from the pollution and crime of Harlem. She knew her father, who still talked wistfully about the old farm in South Carolina, would especially enjoy being out of the city.

In her excitement Althea got overconfident, and she turned down the Harlem Globetrotters' offer to tour overseas the next year. Instead, she tried organizing her own pro basketball-tennis tour, thinking she'd make even more money that way. But the profits depended on how big the audiences were. Without the draw of the Harlem Globetrotters, hardly anyone came. Althea lost money so fast that she had to cancel her tour after three months. In less than a year she'd gone from feeling like a wealthy woman to sinking almost $25,000 into debt.

Fortunately Althea had already signed a contract with the Ward Baking Company to do public relations work for them. They sponsored her to travel around the country creating goodwill for their products, such as Tip-Top Bread. She spoke on TV and radio, at schools and charity benefits. Her usual talk was the story of her own life, from street kid in Harlem to world-famous tennis champion. Althea especially liked talking to young people. Maybe, she hoped, the story of her success would give a boost to some other struggling girl or boy.

In front of audiences Althea was enthusiastic. But alone in her hotel room, she stared at the ceiling and brooded. Was this where her years of hard work and single-minded determination had landed her? She didn't seem to have any purpose in life, other than paying off her enormous debts. She spent most of her time by herself, getting from one city to another.

After two years of touring for the Ward Baking Company and brooding, Althea decided to take control of her life. She'd been interested for some time in helping young athletes—kids like her, who didn't have the money or connections to make it on their own in the tennis world. She had a dream of founding the Althea Gibson Academy. But that would take money.

Althea resolved to make her money in professional golf. She was now almost thirty-three, but so what? She'd been a late bloomer in tennis, and that hadn't stopped her. Without even working on her golf game, Althea could hit a ball 250 yards. The more she thought about it and talked to golf pros, the more excited she got about this new sports challenge.

For two years Althea practiced golf steadily, playing from early in the morning until the sun went down. She discovered that the game of golf didn't come quite as naturally to her as tennis had. Althea was used to playing against an opponent in the close-fought game of singles tennis. In golf, she was now playing against herself and the course. It was a lonely game, and it demanded great patience.

After many months of practice, Althea felt she'd found her groove in golf. She began to compete in amateur tournaments. In 1963 she announced her intention to qualify for the Ladies' Professional Golf Association, and she played in seven pro tournaments. Her game wasn't yet good enough for her to qualify as a professional, but she'd known this would be another practice year. In 1964, she vowed, she'd either qualify or quit.

As if becoming a professional golf player weren't enough of a challenge, Althea had to struggle against racial prejudice in this sport too. With all the progress in race relations since Althea's ATA days, there were still many country clubs where black people were not allowed. At one of the clubs hosting an LPGA tournament, the management told her that she could play on the golf course, but she couldn't use the women's locker room. Althea calmly changed her shoes in the parking lot—and played so well in the tournament that she was now qualified for her pro card.

Later, another country club refused to let Althea play at all. But the LPGA refused to go along with such blatant racism. They moved that tournament to a public golf course.

Meanwhile, in 1965 Althea married Will Darben. He was her friend Rosemary's brother, one of the family who'd "adopted" her in the early 1950s. He'd been a good friend and off-and-on boyfriend of Althea's for fifteen years. Will had suggested marriage before, but until now she had always turned him down.

In May 1967 Althea's father died of a sudden illness. As she grieved with her family, she was glad that at least Dush Gibson had lived to see her become a champion. And although she hadn't done as much for her family as she wanted to, at least she'd bought them a nice house in a place where they could breathe fresh air. Thanks to Althea, her father had spent his last few years in a home surrounded by blue sky and green grass.

Payback for Althea

Althea Gibson wrote another book, published in 1968, about her life since quitting tennis. The title, *So Much to Live For*, came from a song she often performed. At this point she still had high hopes for her golf career.

Althea stuck with professional golf until 1971, playing in 171 tournaments. She didn't win any of them, and the money she made hadn't even covered her expenses. She hated to quit, but at the age of forty-three, it seemed like time to say she'd tried her best.

At least she could be proud of one of her achievements in golf: She'd paved the way, as she had in tennis, for other African-American players to come.

As another milestone for Althea in 1971, she was inducted into the Tennis Hall of Fame in Newport, Rhode Island. Times had changed. In the 1970s tennis was a wildly popular sport. In addition, players who made money playing tennis were no longer looked down upon. In 1968 the U.S. National Championships had become the U.S. Open, open to professionals as well as amateurs.

Black athletes were much better accepted than when Althea was struggling to make her mark. Another African-American player, Arthur Ashe, had won the first U.S. Open in 1968. Ashe was also a student of Althea's mentor Dr. Johnson.

Althea could now make a living as a professional tennis teacher. She took a job as a teaching pro at a club in New Jersey, and then she opened her own indoor tennis club. She especially liked working with young people. Years later, they would remember her kindness and patience, as well as her good advice. "Be who you are," she told one girl, "and let your racquet do the talking."

Another change in the tennis world was that women were now able to earn big money. Billie Jean King, inspired as a teenager by Althea's story in *I Always Wanted to Be Somebody*, had won the U. S. championship four times and Wimbledon six times. In 1971 King became the first woman athlete to earn $100,000 in one year.

Althea decided to try a comeback in tennis in 1973. But when she applied to play in the U.S. Open, the officials told her she would have to qualify first. Althea Gibson, former world champion of women's tennis, would have to play preliminary rounds to prove she could still compete. She felt insulted, and her confidence was shaken. What if she didn't do well in the qualifying matches? She gave up the idea.

In 1975 Althea and Will Darben were divorced. That same year, she took a job as recreation director of the city of East Orange, New Jersey. Shortly afterward she was appointed athletic commissioner of the state of New Jersey, serving until 1977. She was the first woman in the United States to serve in this kind of position.

Fittingly, Althea made her home in East Orange. It was the Orange Lawn Tennis Club in neighboring South Orange that had given Althea her first chance, in 1950, to play in a USLTA grass court tournament. Of course, "lawn tennis" was now an outdated term, since only a few tournaments were played on grass in the seventies. In 1975 the USLTA had officially changed its name to USTA.

Althea's career in athletic competition might be over, but not her life in tennis. She taught tennis; she traveled to give tennis clinics and lectures. She also played in charity events such as the Women's Tennis Classic. When she played against Chris Evert, tennis champion of the 1970s, Evert commented, "Althea's service is the strongest of any woman playing today."

Althea found it deeply satisfying to help younger athletes, especially girls. She passed on the good advice that her coaches had given her. "Find the toughest opponents you can," she urged her students, "and play them until you beat them. They'll force you to play your best—and to get even better."

At her tennis camp in 1980, Althea worked with a promising African-American girl from Houston, Zina Garrison. Zina was in awe of the former champion, with her royal bearing and deep, rich voice. From Althea and the other pros at the camp, the young tennis player learned how important a winning state of mind was to her tennis game.

That August, Althea's coaching paid off for

Zina. She entered the ATA's national tournament and won. At sixteen, she was the youngest player ever to win the ATA women's singles. Althea was delighted to be the one to present the trophy to Zina.

Zina continued to progress, reaching the semifinals at Wimbledon in 1984. She was the first black woman since Althea Gibson—almost thirty years before!—to play at Wimbledon. During the next several years, Zina called Althea at least once a month to get encouragement and talk over her tennis game. "You've got to put more pop in your serve," Althea told Zina.

In 1990 Zina returned to Wimbledon. and Althea also came and watched the tournament from the royal box. This year Zina got as far as the finals, playing Martina Navratilova for the championship. In the locker room before the match, Althea told Zina, "I'm proud to witness history in the making."

In 1991, just a few months before that year's Wimbledon, Alice Marble died. Althea spoke on a radio program honoring her first tennis role model. Althea Gibson herself was sixty-three, and sadly, her own health had been going downhill since the late 1970s.

For a former champion athlete, used to being in superb condition, this was especially hard to bear. Althea had severe arthritis, which made it difficult and painful to move. In 1995 she had a stroke. She also suffered from a degenerative disease, but she wouldn't talk about it, even with friends. More and more, she kept to herself.

Althea had always taken pride in paying her own way, and now she was too proud to let people know how poor she was. She had trouble paying her bills. One time, the heat in her apartment was turned off.

Finally, in September 1996 Angela Buxton visited her old friend and saw just how poor and sick Althea was. She told a reporter for *Inside Tennis* how the former world champion was living now. Angela knew that Althea would rather keep her dignity than get help, but she didn't agree. It didn't seem right that this woman, a hero to so many, was just getting by on her small Social Security pension.

Hearing about Althea's need, Zina Garrison sent her money. The Mt. Tamalpais Racquet Club in Marin, California, hosted a benefit to raise money for Althea. They named the event "Thanks, Althea." One speaker told the audience, "Althea, this is not charity. This is payback."

In 1997 the Arthur Ashe Stadium opened at the United States Tennis Association Center in New York. The stadium was dedicated to the memory of Arthur Ashe, the black tennis champion who had died in 1993. Althea Gibson was also honored at the dedication ceremony on August 25. She wasn't well enough to attend, but she watched on TV. It was Althea's seventieth birthday, as well as the fortieth anniversary of her first championship at the USLTA nationals at Forest Hills.

The present USTA Center was near the site of the World's Fair grounds of 1939. Althea smiled, remembering riding the bike to that fair with her buddy Charles, more than sixty years ago. That was the first time Althea—or just about anyone else—had seen a television set. TV had come a long way, from that odd little machine on exhibit in the RCA Pavilion to the ordinary color TV set Althea was watching today.

Likewise, the USTA had come a long way since the time when allowing black players to compete was not even discussed. The ATA still did important work in encouraging African-American tennis players, especially

disadvantaged youth. But other tennis orga-
nizations also helped to bring more young
minority players into the game. In 1991 the
USTA had established a Multicultural Parti-
cipation Committee in an effort to reach out
to minorities.

Ill as she was these days, Althea still kept
track of young tennis players, watching their
matches on TV. Venus Williams and her sister
Serena, both tall, strong African-American
women, were rising young stars in the 1990s.
Venus sometimes talked to Althea on the
phone, discussing her tennis game. "Move
your feet," Althea advised her.

Many of Althea's friends tried to keep
in touch, but she was too proud to let most
of them know how she'd gone downhill.
David Dinkins, a tennis fan and mayor of
New York from 1989 to 1993, called her
every year on her birthday. "Champ?" he'd
say to her answering machine. "Pick up if

you're there." She did not pick up. She had difficulty in talking, because of her illness.

Back in the 1960s, Althea had dreamed of creating an organization to help inner-city young people through sports. Now she and a friend, Frances Clayton Gray, launched the Althea Gibson Foundation. This organization would find and encourage urban youth with a talent for tennis or golf.

In 1999 the Althea Gibson Early Childhood Education Academy, for children six years old and younger, was opened in East Orange. Some of the residents at the dedication thought their famous neighbor had already passed away, because they never saw her. The blinds in her apartment were kept lowered.

Shortly after her seventy-sixth birthday, in September 2003, Althea died of respiratory failure. There was an outpouring of tributes.

In Clarendon County, South Carolina, where Dush and Annie Gibson had once scratched out a bare living in the cotton fields, the Manning High School Tennis Complex had been named after Althea Gibson. Now bouquets of flowers decorated the memorial plaque on the tennis courts.

Billie Jean King, women's tennis champion of the 1960s, remembered when she was thirteen and first saw Althea Gibson play. "My heart was pounding. I thought, geez, I hope I can play like that someday."

Venus Williams, winner of Wimbledon and the U.S. Open in both 2000 and 2001, said, "Her accomplishments set the stage for my success."

Althea Gibson's life was a fierce struggle against poverty and racial injustice. She enjoyed two years of triumph at the pinnacle of the tennis world, but only after years of hard work and many disappointments. Sadly, she never received as much money as she deserved for her achievements. Nor did she receive the recognition she deserved, until after her death. But Althea more than fulfilled the desire she had expressed in 1958, when she announced her retirement from tennis: "I hope that I have accomplished just one thing: that I have been a credit to tennis and my country."

For More Information

Gibson, Althea, ed. by Ed Fitzgerald,
   I Always Wanted to Be Somebody.
   Harper & Row, 1958.
   Althea's own frank and lively story of her life,
   up to her second Wimbledon victory.

Biracree, Tom,
   Althea Gibson, Tennis Champion.
   American Women of Achievement series,
   Chelsea House Publishers, 1989.
   This book contains many photographs of
   Althea, as well as of the places and people
   in her life.

Gray, Frances Clayton and Yanick Rice Lamb,
   *Born to Win: The Authorized Biography of
   Althea Gibson*.
   John Wiley & Sons, Inc., 2004.
   This biography is coauthored by Frances

Clayton Gray, a friend of Althea's and executor of her estate. It contains much previously unpublished information and forty rare photographs.

On the Internet

Images from the 1939 New York World's Fair Web site
http://www2.sjsu.edu/faculty/wooda/nywf.html

Museum of the City of New York Web site: Photographs of Harlem in the 1930s and 1940s
http://www.mcny.org/Exhibitions/abbott/n59page.htm

The Official Site of Sugar Ray Robinson—Biography

http://www.cmgww.com/sports/robinson/
biography.html

The All England Lawn Tennis and Croquet
Club (the official Wimbledon Web site)
http://www.wimbledon.org/en_GB/index.
html

The Web page of the Museum Galleries at
the International Tennis Hall of Fame in
Newport, RI
http://www.tennisfame.com/museum.html

For Adult Readers

Ashe, Arthur R., Jr.,
A Hard Road to Glory: A History of the
African-American Athlete, 1919–1945 (vol. 2).
Warner Books, Inc., 1988.
A thorough history of black players in several

sports, and biographical sketches of major athletes.

King, Billie Jean, and Cynthia Starr,
We Have *Come a Long Way: The Story of Women's Tennis.*
McGraw-Hill, 1988.
Much good information on the careers of Althea and other major women tennis players whose lives intersected with hers.

Schoenfeld, Bruce,
The Match: Althea Gibson & Angela Buxton: How Two Outsiders—One Black, the Other Jewish—Forged a Friendship and Made Sports History.
Amistad Press, 2004.
An evenhanded, often touching account of Althea's adult life and her special friendship with another top woman tennis player of the 1950s.